MW00415009

"*Lead Them to Jesus* provides gospel-centered answers to the most common questions facing anyone in youth ministry. I'm planning to use this book to train all of our future youth leaders!"

Drew Hill, Pastor; award-winning author of *Alongside: Loving Teenagers with the Gospel*

"Mike has done a great service to the church with this book. *Lead Them to Jesus* is more than good—it's essential reading. His overarching sections on biblical truths and practical helps will make this a reference book for youth workers for years to come. I plan to revisit the material consistently."

John Perritt, Director of Resources, Reformed Youth Ministries; author of *Mark: How Jesus Changes Everything*; editor for the Track series for students; host of *The Local Youth Worker* podcast

"For every parent who has struggled to answer your teen's theological questions or give a gospel response to postmodern issues, this book is as much for you as it is for youth workers! A reference book you will want to keep handy!"

Kristen Hatton, Author of *The Gospel Centered Life in Exodus, Face Time,* and *Get Your Story Straight*

"*Lead Them to Jesus* is a great and timely resource. This book will equip leaders with basic biblical truths and walk them through everything from leading students to Christ all the way to discussing a theology of suffering. Often you can find resources that address the theological or the practical, but this resource combines both orthodoxy and orthopraxy, allowing leaders to grow in their walks while preparing them to lead others to do the same."

Shane Pruitt, National Next Gen Director, North American Mission Board (NAMB); author of *9 Common Lies Christians Believe*

"*Lead Them to Jesus* helps pastors and youth ministers equip and disciple their youth ministry team. Mike combines basic training in biblical doctrine with a gospel-centered philosophy of ministry and a practical mindset. The chapters that help youth workers care for students who doubt or struggle with biblical sexuality are particularly helpful. I can imagine a student ministry team huddling before their weekly gatherings to discuss a chapter each week."

Jared Kennedy, Author of *God Made Me for Worship* and *The Beginner's Gospel Story Bible*; managing editor of Gospel-Centered Family

"For many who work with young people, the constant barrage of questions and doubts from teenagers about Christianity, along with the practical struggles of youth ministry, can be wearisome and discouraging. Mike McGarry has written a thorough, clear, and remarkably helpful handbook to help address those discouragements head on. *Lead Them to Jesus* is the exact resource every youth worker needs in ministry."

Shelby Abbott, Author of *DoubtLess* and *Pressure Points*; speaker; campus minister

"I cannot recommend this volume highly enough. Useful, compassionate, clear, and engaging, this is one book I will be passing out to volunteers and students for many years to come."

Robin Barfield, Associate Minister, Christ Church, Wharton, UK; visiting lecturer, Oak Hill College and Union School of Theology

"Volunteer leaders form the backbone of any healthy student ministry. Unfortunately, many of these leaders feel ill-equipped to engage students with the truths of Scripture and the gospel of Jesus Christ. In his book, *Lead Them to Jesus: A Handbook for Youth Workers*, Mike McGarry offers youth workers answers to critical questions that students ask and presents helpful, practical skills to help them navigate student ministry."

Tim McKnight, Director of the Global Center for Youth Ministry; associate professor of youth ministry and missions, Anderson University

"If you ever wanted an introductory handbook to just about everything you'll need to know in youth ministry, then this is that book! *Lead Them to Jesus* is the book I wish I was given years ago."

Tim Gough, Author of *Rebooted: Reclaiming Youth Ministry for the Long Haul*; director of Llandudno Youth for Christ, Wales

"*Lead Them to Jesus* is an outstanding resource for youth leaders. Mike McGarry offers short commentaries on forty important issues and tasks in youth ministry, and he doesn't shy away from hot-button issues! This is a great handbook for providing biblical answers to the challenging questions of teenagers and learning to carry out the essential tasks of youth ministry."

Mark W. Cannister, Professor of Christian Ministries, Gordon College

"There is a dearth of helpful, gospel-centered resources available to youth ministers fighting the good fight for today's teenagers. I am so grateful for longtime youth pastor Mike McGarry and his latest book, *Lead Them to Jesus*. I pray that this book finds its way into the hands of pastors and volunteers across the world."

Charlotte Getz, Editor-in-chief, Rooted Ministry

"This is the book I wish I had when I started out in youth ministry. It deals winsomely with some of the most significant theological issues that youth pastors will face when working with teenagers, as well as offering excellent practical advice for running a regular youth ministry. I will be putting this into the hands of my team."

Peter Wright, Youth Worker, Hill Street Presbyterian Church; tutor with Crosslands

"For youth workers wanting to help teens find answers to the hard questions of faith and life, Mike is a wonderful guide and this book is an amazing map. If you're a youth worker, you need a copy."

Christopher Talbot, Instructor of Ministry, Welch College; author of *Remodeling Youth Ministry: A Biblical Blueprint for Ministering to Students*

"Most resources for youth ministry workers prize either theology or practical tips over the other, but anyone serving in youth ministry knows that both are required to see growing disciples and engaged students, in addition to helping volunteers to feel supported and equipped to serve well. If you are a minister, volunteer, church leader, teacher, or even parent of a teenager in youth ministry, you need to own this book."

Rebecca Heck, Codirector of Student Ministry, Intown Community Church, Atlanta, GA

"This is the book that youth ministry has desperately needed! It is a doctrinally rich and practically thorough resource for those caring for young people in the local church. It will be one of the essential go-to books for anyone concerned to nurture the next generation for Jesus."

Melanie Lacy, Executive Director, Growing Young Disciples

"*Lead Them to Jesus* is the go-to resource for new youth workers and volunteers. Mike McGarry unites theology and practical skills into one resource to equip the next generation of youth workers. Every team would benefit from reading and discussing this book together."

Doug Franklin, President, LeaderTreks Youth Ministry

"I have so often wished there were a book equipping laypeople for gospel ministry to teenagers, a resource that would help adults to think biblically, while inspiring their courage to dive into the messy, beautiful work of walking with middle and high school students. *Lead Them to Jesus* is the book I've long hoped for, and I can't wait to give it to every leader in our ministry. Mike speaks both theologically and practically to the concerns of youth workers, showing how the cross and resurrection of Jesus shapes every last one."

Chelsea Kingston Erickson, Pastor of Youth and Families, First Congregational Church of Hamilton, MA

"What a gift this is for youth workers who want to somehow give their volunteers all the practical tips, sage advice, critical warnings, and theological foundations that are necessary for biblical youth ministry! The format is just right for volunteers: short enough to engage, but deep enough to nurture and teach. I highly recommend it!"

Duffy Robbins, Professor of Christian Ministries, Grove City College, Grove City, PA

"*Lead Them to Jesus* is a book that youth pastors of any experience level will pull off the shelf over and over again. McGarry has given youth pastors a true gift in this theologically rich, biblically sound handbook."

Cameron Cole, Founding Chairman of Rooted; coeditor of *Gospel-Centered Youth Ministry* and *The Jesus I Wish I Knew in High School*; author of *Therefore I Have Hope*

"Are you ready to aim teenagers and their parents toward Jesus and his church? *Lead Them to Jesus* is one of the resources that will help you to move in this direction."

Timothy Paul Jones, C. Edwin Gheens Chair of Christian Ministry, The Southern Baptist Theological Seminary; author of *Family Ministry Field Guide*; editor of *Perspectives on Family Ministry*

"In one concise resource, Mike McGarry has provided a wealth of theological and practical guidance for youth workers, both those with and without formal training. I cannot recommend this resource highly enough!"

Andy Blanks, Cofounder and publisher, YM360

"In a day and age where youth workers must navigate a growing volume of cultural confusion, there is an urgent parallel need for youth ministry clarity. I'm grateful to Mike for this most helpful contribution to our youth ministry world."

Walt Mueller, Center for Parent/Youth Understanding

LEAD THEM TO JESUS

A Handbook for Youth Workers

Mike McGarry

New
Growth
Press
newgrowthpress.com

New Growth Press, Greensboro, NC 27404
newgrowthpress.com
Copyright © 2021 by Mike McGarry

All rights reserved. No part of this publication may be reproduced, stored in a retrieval system, or transmitted in any form by any means, electronic, mechanical, photocopy, recording, or otherwise, without the prior permission of the publisher, except as provided by USA copyright law.

Unless otherwise indicated, all Scripture quotations are from the ESV® Bible (The Holy Bible, English Standard Version®). ESV® Text Edition: 2016. Copyright © 2001 by Crossway, a publishing ministry of Good News Publishers. Used by permission. All rights reserved.

Scripture quotations labeled (NIV) are taken from the Holy Bible, New International Version®, NIV®. Copyright © 1973, 1978, 1984, 2011 by Biblica, Inc.® Used by permission. All rights reserved worldwide.

Cover Design: Faceout Books, faceoutstudio.com
Interior Design and Typesetting: Gretchen Logterman

ISBN: 978-1-64507-130-3 (Print)
ISBN: 978-1-64507-131-0 (eBook)

Library of Congress Cataloging-in-Publication Data

Names: McGarry, Mike, 1980- author.
Title: Lead them to Jesus : a handbook for youth workers / Mike McGarry.
Description: Greensboro, NC : New Growth Press, [2021] | Includes
   bibliographical references. | Summary: "Veteran youth pastor Mike
   McGarry offers a practical, comprehensive tool to jumpstart your youth
   ministry and help youth workers with biblical answers to the tough
   questions students ask"-- Provided by publisher.
Identifiers: LCCN 2020057252 (print) | LCCN 2020057253 (ebook) | ISBN
   9781645071303 (trade paperback) | ISBN 9781645071310 (ebook)
Subjects: LCSH: Church work with teenagers--Handbooks, manuals, etc. |
   Church work with youth--Handbooks, manuals, etc.
Classification: LCC BV4447 .M3725 2021 (print) | LCC BV4447 (ebook) | DDC
   259/.23--dc23
LC record available at https://lccn.loc.gov/2020057252
LC ebook record available at https://lccn.loc.gov/2020057253

Printed in Canada

28 27 26 25 24 23 22 21   1 2 3 4 5

For the youth workers at South Shore Baptist Church.
I wrote this book for you.

Contents

Section 2: Practical Help for Youth Workers

Introduction

As I write, there is a meme going around on the Facebook groups for youth workers. It shows an overwhelmed-looking young man, and is captioned, "I don't know what I'm doing . . . but I'm figuring it out as I go!" It got a lot of likes and comments. People resonate with its message.

This book is written so you won't.

Most youth workers are volunteers who make generous sacrifices of their time, emotions, and money in order to lead students to Jesus. They use their vacation time to go on camps, retreats, and mission trips with hormonal teenagers (have you ever smelled a middle-school boys' cabin after two days?). In their passion for serving students, they are often plugged into a ministry wherever there's the greatest need, given a few quick pointers on what to do, and then set loose with a vague promise of training. Too often, this has been my own practice with youth workers, and it doesn't set them up for long-term, joyful service.

The idea for this book came from my own need for it. After serving in the same church for more than a decade, I began searching for resources to equip my new team of youth workers. The handbooks I found were either outdated or failed to help youth workers see how the gospel shapes each topic addressed, and my favorite youth ministry blogs weren't comprehensive enough. Resources seemed to provide youth workers with a solid theology for ministry or with practical skills, but not both. As I wrote down a list of topics I wanted to talk about with my youth workers, I realized I had a good table of contents for a resource that could help more than just my own team. This book brings theology and practice together with a singular vision for gospel-centered youth ministry.

This is a natural follow-up to my previous book, *A Biblical Theology of Youth Ministry: Teenagers in the Life of the Church* (Randall House Academic, 2019). That first book tells about a biblical theology for youth ministry. This book shows what that actually looks like. It is written to give you a biblical and practical resource that will help you build your ministry to teenagers around the gospel.

Most youth workers who preach the gospel and hold to historic Christian doctrines consider themselves gospel-centered. While these practices are essential, they do not automatically make a minister or a ministry "gospel-centered." While other ministries might be gospel-absent, these are simply gospel-present. Gospel-centered youth ministry is built on the firm conviction that the gospel should directly inform every facet of the youth ministry. To that end, this book presents clear guidance on ways the gospel shapes not only how to teach biblical sexuality and theology, but also how it shapes mission trips, game time, parent ministry, and the youth group calendar.

Gospel-centered youth workers want to lead students to Jesus, regardless of the topic or event. This book is divided into two sections to help you accomplish that mission. The first equips youth workers to answer questions teens often have about God and the Bible. The second is a guide to the practical tasks of operating a youth ministry.

SECTION ONE: BIBLICAL ANSWERS FOR YOUTH WORKERS

Theology drives methodology. Many have said it, and it's true. What we believe about God, salvation, and the Bible has a very real impact on the way we minister to students. For this reason, there are some important doctrines that youth workers should be equipped to discuss with students. After all, how can we help students grapple with who God is if we ourselves don't have a basic understanding of the Trinity? Or how can we help students endure suffering if we have a thin view of why God allows suffering to exist?

If you want to make lifelong disciples, social media and merely "hanging out" isn't going to cut it. You need to be prepared to go deep with students about what they believe and why, and you can't take them where you've never gone.

This book assumes that you, as a volunteer youth worker, have never received formal education in biblical studies or theology. Please do not avoid section 1 even if you find the theology difficult at times. The topics covered in this section will equip you to grow as a disciple maker, even as your own doctrinal understanding is stretched.

Section Two: Practical Help for Youth Workers

This second half of the book offers practical skills I have learned over fifteen years in ministry and countless conversations with fellow youth pastors. In the midst of its practical counsel, this section will keep showing the ways the gospel shapes every facet of youth ministry. As I highlight repeatedly throughout this book, the gospel is more than an evangelism tool. It is the lifeblood of the entire Christian experience. Without the gospel, everything else we have to offer students might be fun, but it's ultimately futile. The gospel gives life and joy and hope to the way we play games, address conflict, partner with parents, integrate students into the life of the church, or talk about sex.

The gospel truly is good news of great joy for all people. May it fill your soul with joy as you lead students to Jesus.

Starting Point: What Is the Gospel?

T he gospel is the best news in the history of creation. And yet, even as church kids may be so familiar with some parts of the gospel that they stop listening to it, and even though some could tell you that *gospel* means "good news," most still struggle to articulate what that good news actually is. It is "good news of a great joy that will be for all the people" (Luke 2:10), but maybe the reason students are so fuzzy on the gospel is because we are too. The gospel is so much more than an evangelistic message that ushers people into heaven. Instead, it's more like the heart transplant that brings the Christian to life and keeps him alive every single day.

GETTING CLEAR ON THE GOSPEL

It is impossible to preach the gospel without highlighting the death and resurrection of Jesus Christ. Jesus lived a sinless life, died a painful death as the substitute for all of God's children, rose from the grave in victory over sin and death, and will return to complete both his judgment of sin and the salvation of his people. This is good news for every generation, and it is worthy of being proclaimed every chance we get. I have heard many evangelistic ministries hold out to students the promises of the gospel (especially salvation from sin and the love of God) while barely mentioning the cross and resurrection. At these types of youth events, a call to repentance is frequently absent or severely downplayed in order to proclaim the love and mercy of God to students who are hurting. But talking about the love and grace of God is not the same thing as presenting the gospel. Faithful Jews and Muslims can talk about God's love! Christian youth workers need to remember that neglecting to preach the whole gospel out of a desire to keep the gospel simple and clear will only lead students to shallow faith that fails to grasp the full breadth and power of their salvation.

At its heart, the gospel is the proclamation that God saves sinners through Jesus Christ. It is not a "new law" or a revision of the Ten Commandments. It is not a philosophy to grasp, or even a theology to unlock. Instead, it is the grace of God that sinners receive by faith. Because of the gospel, sinners have become children of God, set free from bondage to sin and guilt and shame, and they have a new destiny: eternal joy in the presence of God, their heavenly Father. This, my friends, is good news indeed!

The gospel of grace lies at the heart of everything youth workers are trying to accomplish. There is nothing the church has to offer students that the world can't match—apart from the gospel. Dig deeply into it, plumbing the depths of its many facets throughout the entire Bible. Also keep your own heart warmed toward the majesty and mystery of this good news, lest it become dry and routine to both you and the students you serve.

REVISITING HOW WE PRESENT THE GOSPEL TO STUDENTS

There are two approaches to gospel proclamation that I believe need to be revisited: one that crams Jesus down students' throats, and another that attempts to "preach the gospel without words." Although they appear to be opposite approaches, they are actually different sides of the same coin. Both try to compel a genuine profession of faith. This means that, at best, these approaches only produce false converts who conform to the externals of Christianity for a while.

The force-feeding approach fails because we're all the same in this regard: when someone crams something down your throat, you're probably going to vomit it out even if it's good for you. We know this, but some youth workers and parents continue to do it anyway. Many church kids have not rejected Jesus as much as they've rejected him being forced upon them through pressure to think and behave Christianly even if their heart isn't in it. Their zealous parents and youth workers misunderstand the gospel because good news of great joy doesn't need to be forced; it simply needs to be announced. The gospel must take root in the heart before it changes students' behavior. Proclaim the death and resurrection of Jesus Christ with confidence, and trust the Holy Spirit to do the work only he can do.

The "preach without words" approach falls short because none of us can *be* the gospel. The gospel is the announcement of God's grace poured out on sinners through the life, death, resurrection, and eventual return of Jesus Christ. When Christians live in a way that reflects the gracious love of God, it may warm nonbelievers toward hearing the gospel. But they still need to *hear* it, because it's news about who Jesus is and what he's done—not about what we have done to love them. So let's drop the talk about "being the gospel" and renew our commitment to being changed by the gospel, loving others as Christ loved us, and telling them what God has done through Jesus.

More Than an Evangelistic Message

The gospel is so much more than just a message that initially calls sinners to trust in Jesus for salvation and new life. The gospel of grace lies at the heart of our whole salvation: justification (our righteous standing with God), sanctification (our growth in holiness), and glorification (our coming perfection). And yet, with sanctification it is common for discipleship ministries to overlook the centrality of the gospel. Instead, they merely share practical counsel for students about how they can work to become more like Christ. This usually happens with good intentions, but it leads students into works-righteousness rather than daily dependence on the Spirit. As the apostle Paul cried out in Galatians 3:3, "Are you so foolish? Having begun by the Spirit, are you now being perfected by the flesh?"

Theologians often refer to four chapters of salvation history: creation, fall, redemption, and glorification. This is helpful for youth workers to remember because it lets us locate where students are in their walk with Christ. Of course, none of us are still in the creation chapter, and no one currently in your youth group has already been glorified. So every student you meet is marked by either the fall or redemption. Students who have not professed faith in Christ and repented of their sin are still marked by the fall—they do not belong to Christ and they need to hear and believe the gospel. But those who have confessed their sin and confessed Christ Jesus as Lord and have professed their desire to turn from sin and follow Jesus (repentance) are marked by redemption. Their lives been transformed by the grace they have received and by the power of the indwelling Holy Spirit as they hear and grow in the gospel. This is why the gospel is the heartbeat that drives your entire ministry to students.

You must ask yourself this: Do you really believe the gospel is good news of great joy, or do you think it's just okay? Students can tell when your heart is lukewarm toward the gospel. If you proclaim the gospel from your heels, holding back from presenting it with joyful enthusiasm because you aren't sure it's all that great, they can tell. The single best thing you can do for your ministry is to continually warm your own heart by the life-giving message of the gospel. If the gospel is just okay news, then it's on a level playing field with any number of other life-improving philosophies. But if it's true that God really does save sinners through Jesus, and that it's all a work of grace, then it really is good news!

Biblical Truths for Youth Workers

1

How Do I Become a Christian?

The gospel is the proclamation of the good news that God saves sinners through Jesus Christ. Inherent in this message is an invitation to come and be saved. But what does that mean, and how can youth workers help an interested student who is not a Christian become one?

Not every Christian knows when they became a Christian, and that's okay. Following Jesus is about more than a singular moment when someone prays a prayer; it's about living as a dearly loved child of God who has received grace through faith in Jesus who lived, died, rose again, and will return one day. That being said, it is important for youth workers to know how to lead students who are either "on the fence" or are self-professed non-Christians into a new life with Christ.

HELP STUDENTS COUNT THE COST

In group settings where nonbelieving students are hearing the gospel, some for the very first time, it's crucial to encourage students to count the cost of becoming a Christian as you proclaim the good news of Jesus Christ. Students who profess faith in Christ without knowing that he calls us to repentance, personal holiness, and persecution will likely fall away when their newfound faith becomes inconvenient. Doing this in one-on-one settings is probably easier because you will be able to speak specifically to that student, raising questions and issues they need to consider. But in large-group ministry, especially in evangelistic settings, this concern is easily overlooked.

You see, the gospel is more than an invitation to find deep joy and receive eternal life. It's also an invitation to begin life as a child of God *today*. And that life is lived in a world that hated, betrayed, and killed the Son of God on the cross. We should expect a measure of opposition as well. Many students have professed faith at an evangelistic retreat only to walk away from the faith when life got difficult. While we want to be cautious of scaring away students who are considering Christ (because what we receive through grace immeasurably outweighs what we sacrifice for Christ), it is dishonest to minimize the difficult aspects of the Christian life until after they have decided to become a Christian.

Should We Use the "Sinner's Prayer"?

Potential converts are sometimes asked to pray a "sinner's prayer" that usually sounds something like this: "Dear God, I confess that I am a sinner and cannot save myself. Please forgive me of my sin through Jesus Christ's death and resurrection and give me new life in him. Amen." Many who have attended an evangelistic ministry and then prayed the prayer consider themselves Christians even though they have never repented of their sin. Perhaps they confessed their sin and their need for salvation, but they did not turn from sin and cast their faith onto Christ. In many cases, teenagers pray this prayer every year at camp because it didn't seem to produce any lasting change previously. The fault is not entirely in the sinner's prayer, per se, as much as in a weak understanding of conversion and evangelism. True faith and repentance are an inner response of the heart to the grace of Christ, not an external prayer.

Due to the misuses of conversion prayers, many pastors hesitate to encourage them at all. For sure, they are not mandatory.

But when sinners confess their sin and profess faith in Jesus Christ, prayer is an appropriate way to express that newfound faith. At such times, leading them in prayer is a faithful way to teach them about the importance of prayer for their new life in Christ. You will want to emphasize that the power is not in praying any particular prayer, but in the faithfulness of the heavenly Father who has secured salvation through his Son, has adopted the new Christian through the indwelling Holy Spirit, and now loves to hear from his child.

How to Lead a Student to Saving Faith

1. **Trust God.** Salvation is the work of God. You cannot save anyone. Relieve yourself from the need to give a perfect answer for every question. God is already at work in each person who believes, and he will use your imperfect gospel presentations to lead students to himself.
2. **Confidently proclaim the gospel.** Romans 6:23 is a helpful verse: "For the wages of sin is death, but the free gift of God is eternal life in Christ Jesus our Lord." Through faith in Jesus, by his virgin birth, sinless life, substitutionary death, bodily resurrection, glorious ascension, and eventual return, we have received adoption as holy and beloved children of God. That is God's plan of salvation, and it is indeed good news of great joy for all people. Proclaim it widely with confidence.
3. **Invite the student to repent of sin.** If students cannot identify their specific need for salvation, and if they do not repent of their sin, then they do not want to be a Christian—they simply want the benefits of Christ. Repentance goes deeper than mere confession. Confession means "to admit," while repentance means "to change your mind" or "to turn around." When students confess their sin but do not repent, they are simply acknowledging their sin without expressing any desire for God to change them. Encourage students to pray, confessing their sin, professing faith in Jesus Christ, and asking the Lord for the grace to live as a disciple of Jesus.

4. **Affirm the grace of God.** God's grace is eternally greater than our imperfect faith and half-hearted repentance. No one confesses or repents perfectly. Every student will stumble their way through conversion—and that's the beauty of it. Highlight the power of grace to remove guilt and shame and to give a new heart and identity to each person who believes.

5. **Disciple the student or find someone who will.** The purpose of evangelism is not to give students a free ticket to heaven when they die, hoping they don't lose it along the way. Evangelism that does not consider how to help students meaningfully grow in their new identity as a child of God is both irresponsible and unbiblical. Follow up with students to ensure someone is helping them discover how to live their new life in Christ.

2

Can I Trust and Understand the Bible?

"The Bible was put together hundreds of years after Jesus lived."

"What good can a two-thousand-year-old book be for today's world?"

"That's just your interpretation."

These are statements you've likely heard from students who are questioning the Bible. You also may have noticed that when students fall away from faith it often begins when they stop viewing the Bible as the inspired and authoritative Word of God. Some merely look for ways to marginalize Scripture in order to live in sin. But others genuinely wrestle with the relevance and reliability of a two-thousand-year-old book.

If the Bible is reliable and trustworthy, then students can have confidence in what it says and they can look to it for wisdom about how to live for the glory of God. But if the Bible is just another book, and if all interpretations are equally valid, then students will have freedom to be their own authority on what is right and wrong, true and false, beautiful and evil.

The historical trustworthiness of Scripture matters because the Bible isn't an instruction manual for life, but God's revelation of himself through the person and work of Jesus Christ.

Christians who lose confidence in the authority and trustwor-thiness of Scripture soon find themselves floundering in faith. Gospel-centered youth workers lead students to Jesus with con-fidence in the Word of God.

ARCHAEOLOGY AFFIRMS THE BIBLE

Each book of the Bible was written with ink on a scroll or codex (a forerunner to the paperback book) and carefully recopied over the centuries. Many ancient copies have since been lost or destroyed, but what we've unearthed gives us an accurate bibli-cal text in the original languages. When historians compare the vast number of ancient copies against other ancient texts that are highly regarded for their insight into the ancient world and consider how few years separate those manuscripts from when the original New Testament letters were written, the historical reliability of the Bible is simply unparalleled.[1] It is unreasonable to expect that we must still have the original biblical documents in order to affirm the authenticity of the Bible. No one would issue a similar demand on any other ancient document.

When compared against other ancient manuscripts, and even against the works of William Shakespeare, scholars' abil-ity to recreate the Bible's original manuscript is unmatched. This is not a matter of opinion, but is objectively true. Plato's *Four Dialogues*, which is read in many introductory philoso-phy courses, has around 200 ancient copies that scholars use to piece together the original book. But when it comes to the New Testament, there are more than 5,800 copies, some of which are dated within a hundred years of the original writings. The reli-ability of the Old Testament was secured by the discovery of the Dead Sea Scrolls in 1946, which showed that the Hebrew text has remained the same over the last two thousand years. Even atheistic archaeologists must admit the Old and New Testaments are historically reliable.

When scholars compare these ancient biblical manuscripts, the differences between texts are almost always about grammar or spellings, and none of the remaining differences affect any central doctrines. This is objective, historic truth—and yet many students hear that the Bible can't be trusted. Addressing this head-on through archaeology and textual criticism assures students that the Bible they hold in their hands is a faithful translation of the original text.

HOW THE BIBLE WAS PUT TOGETHER

Students also might hear conspiracy theories about how some books were included in the Bible while others were left out. But the Bible was not compiled by a select group of elite influencers. Leaders in the early church did not grant authority to certain books to become the Word of God; they affirmed which ones *already* carried authority as being "God-breathed" (2 Timothy 3:16). The identified books were then included in the canon of the New Testament.

During the time of the early church, a "canon" was a rod of papyrus used as a ruler to make accurate and authoritative measurements. This terminology eventually found its way into the church's method for determining whether or not a book "measured up" and belonged within the biblical canon of Holy Scripture. The canon of the Old Testament was already established. Some new books, like the Gospel of Thomas and other gnostic gospels, simply did not measure up to three criteria:

1. **Biblical: God's Word is consistent.** The New Testament must not contradict the Old Testament, because God does not contradict himself. The Old and New Testaments tell one consistent story of God's plan to rescue his children and reestablish his kingdom. The gnostic gospels were dismissed from the canon because their teachings simply did not measure up with biblical teaching, especially on creation and salvation.

2. **Apostolic: Firsthand authorship.** There was early agreement that the teachings of the apostles and other firsthand

witnesses of Jesus's life, death, and resurrection would be prioritized. For instance, Matthew was an apostle who was present for most of what he reported in his gospel. Paul had a direct encounter with Jesus on the road to Damascus and received an apostolic commission. Luke got his information from firsthand sources who walked with Jesus. All the books of the New Testament were written within the lifetime of the apostles and carry the mark of apostolic teaching.

3. **Catholic: Widespread readership.** As books were considered for the canon, churches throughout the Roman Empire (and beyond) were already reading the biblical books as part of their gathered worship. This happened because of the first two criteria: Christians made copies of the Gospels and of letters that reflected gospel authority and carried these to other churches for their benefit. At the time the canon was formalized, Gospels and epistles that were only read in certain areas came up short because they demonstrated too much particularity and too little catholic (universal) appeal. The books of the New Testament were already largely accepted as authoritative by every church throughout the Christian world.

PRACTICAL IMPLICATIONS OF THE BIBLE'S RELIABILITY

- The Bible's reliability gives students confidence that the Bible they read is what the apostles actually wrote. It is common for students to hear that the Bible wasn't created until centuries after Jesus lived and that certain books were left out for political purposes. Without teaching students how the Bible was actually compiled, how are they supposed to affirm the reliability of Scripture?

- It anchors students within a diverse family of faith. Christianity is not a trendy religion that will be outdated by the time they graduate from high school. It is a two-thousand-year-old religion that has stood the test of time, weathered intense persecutions, and united people from every language and culture. When they read the Bible, they can be assured that God's truth is both timeless and relevant to transform their own lives today.

- It reminds students that Jesus really lived, died, and rose from the grave. Christianity is a historically-driven religion. The archaeological reliability of the Bible bolsters students' faith in the truth of the gospel. This is especially important when their faith begins to waver. That's when they need to be anchored in the truth that the Bible is not merely spiritually true but also historically true.

3
What Is the Trinity?

The youth group was painting Alice's house as a service project. She was an older woman with a spitfire personality.
She immediately clicked with a number of our students—and
with me. Over the course of the following year, we had many
conversations about faith and theology, but we regularly seemed
to return to her questions and hesitations about the Trinity. She
simply could not accept that the Father, Son, and Holy Spirit are
one. Finally, I told her, "Alice, if you do not believe that God is
the Trinity, then you are not a Christian."

This might seem like an overstatement, but it's not. How
can anyone consider herself a Christian if she doesn't know who
God is? That was the last conversation about the Trinity we had
for quite a few months. One Sunday after the benediction, she
approached me with a smile across her face and declared, "I get
it. Karl helped me understand. Thank you for helping me see
how important it is to believe God is the Trinity, three in one."

Few areas of Christian theology are more mysterious, or
more important, than the Trinity. The most important differences between the Abrahamic religions—Judaism, Christianity,
and Islam—can be traced back to the Trinity, for it is God the
Son who came to save sinners and the Holy Spirit who adopts
and unites the Christian with God. If someone understands the

Trinity, they have a basic understanding of the most important Christian teachings. It reveals to us who God is (Father, Son, Holy Spirit), what he is like (holy, eternal, sovereign), how he deals with humanity (as Creator, Savior, Advocate, Judge), and what he expects of us (to love and honor one another the way each person of the Trinity loves and honors the others). If a student claims to be a Christian but does not believe in the Trinity, they don't believe in the Jesus of the Bible whom Christians have worshiped for two millennia.

Statements like these can be difficult, especially for youth workers who are ministering to teenagers. Mature adults have a difficult time understanding the Trinity, and it doesn't seem fair to expect teenagers to tackle this most complex of doctrines. Patiently teaching good theology to students, however, makes a significant impact because it shapes their view of God. Don't underestimate what teenagers (yes, even middle school boys) are able to comprehend. The nature of the Trinity is mysterious and beyond our full understanding. This is actually a good thing, because a god whose nature easily makes sense to the human brain must be a pretty small god. God's holiness means that he is "separate" and different from us. But because he is not hiding himself from us, God has revealed enough of his nature to us through the Holy Scriptures for us to understand the following explanation of the Trinity.

The doctrine of the Trinity states that God exists as one God in three persons: God the Father, God the Son, and God the Spirit. Each person of the Trinity is equally and fully God, distinct from the others, and yet they remain just one God. The Bible teaches the Trinity beginning with the days of creation. It tells how God spoke, how his Word was the agent of creation, and how the Spirit hovered over the waters (also consider how John 1:1–18 interprets Genesis 1). Then it tells how God spoke in plural, "Let us make man in our image" (Genesis 1:26), at the creation of humanity. Later, Jesus commands his disciples to baptize new believers "in the name of the Father and of the Son and of the Holy Spirit" (Matthew 28:19). Although the word *Trinity* never appears, the teaching that God is one in three is consistent throughout Scripture, and the New Testament is particularly clear about the divine nature of the three persons.

THREE CORE ELEMENTS OF THE TRINITY

1. **Equal.** The Father is not greater than the Son and the Spirit, nor is any person lesser than any other. God the Son's label of *Son* does not mean he is inferior to the Father, but portrays his role in salvation as the one who is sent by the Father as a Son who represents his family. Similarly, the Holy Spirit is not simply an errand-runner for the Father and Son, but is equal in glory and is worthy of worship. None of the persons were ever created but are equal in honor and eternality. This perfect equality and unity is why Jesus said, "Whoever has seen me has seen the Father" (John 14:9).

2. **Distinct.** Some distinct roles of the Trinity are on display in Ephesians 1:3–14. God the Father "chose us in him before the foundation of the world" (v. 4). The Christian is "in Christ," and God the Son is the one who did the work to accomplish our salvation (vv. 5, 9). And God the Holy Spirit is the one who secures our salvation like a seal that marks a document as something authoritative and legitimate (vv. 13–14). Each person of the Trinity has a particular role, and yet they work in perfect cooperation because they are one.

3. **United.** The Father, Son, and Holy Spirit are one God. The persons of the Trinity do not act in isolation from the others, as if they "go rogue." Instead, they are united as the perfect community from whom we understand what it means to love and honor one another. In John 17:20–26, Jesus's prayer for Christian unity directly flows from his own understanding of the Trinity's communion.

BREAKING DOWN THE BAD ANALOGIES

There is no perfect analogy to help explain the Trinity. The following analogies are common ways people attempt to teach the Trinity to children. Accordingly, it is important for youth workers to know how to correct the ways these misrepresent our triune God.

Egg. This analogy equates the Trinity with the shell, the yolk, and the egg whites all composing one egg. A variation of this uses an apple (the skin, the meat, and the seeds). But this is not like the Trinity, because each component of the egg or apple cannot be said to be an egg. Besides, one usually cracks an egg and discards the shell as useless. And the components of an egg can be separated and are not equal in value.

Water. This analogy compares the Trinity to steam, ice, and water. The Trinity, however, is simultaneously three in one, while a molecule of H_2O must be either water, steam, or ice. Other variations of this emphasize a person's relationships—a man might be a son, a husband, and a father—to express three different types of relationships flowing from the same person. This analogy reflects one of the oldest heresies: that God the Father turned into God the Son who later turned into the Holy Spirit. God is a unity of three persons, not one person with three expressions.

Shamrock. Saint Patrick is the famous originator of this analogy. He used the three leaves of the shamrock to point to the three persons of the Trinity, but this also falls short for the same reason as the egg and apple: each leaf is a component of a shamrock, not fully a shamrock.

The following diagram, dating from the Middle Ages, is a simple (and easy to draw) way to explain the Trinity to students. It highlights that the three persons of the Trinity are equal and united within the Godhead, yet remain distinct from one another.

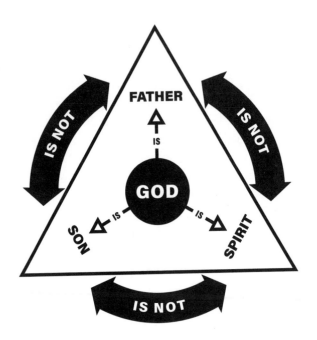

4
Is It Okay to Doubt?

Youth workers shouldn't be surprised when students begin to wrestle with doubt, because faith is a wonderful and mysterious thing. Asking hard questions is a normal part of spiritual development, especially while transitioning from childhood (when you likely believe your parents' worldview because it's all you know) into adulthood (when you develop your own worldview). Many teens experience a strange combination of faith and doubt without knowing how to make sense of it. Even students with genuine faith are plagued by difficult questions:

- What if we did "just happen" and evolved from primordial ooze?
- What if Jesus didn't really say or do the things the Bible says he did?
- How do I know God is even real?
- Why would God allow my parents to get divorced?

Many teenagers who grow up in the church feel pressure to keep their questions to themselves. Or if they do ask hard questions, they feel looked down on and are told to have more faith. Without the freedom to explore their doubts, many walk away from the church—and eventually from faith.

One of my favorite stories in the Gospels comes when Jesus interacts with a man whose son is demon-possessed. When Jesus asks him if he believes Jesus can heal the sick child, he replies, "I believe, help my unbelief!" (Mark 9:24). We need to encourage this kind of honesty in the church.

HARD QUESTIONS AND EASY ANSWERS

God isn't afraid of hard questions. We shouldn't be either. Easy answers are usually offered by well-intentioned believers, but they fail to honestly wrestle with the question and why it is being asked. People are complicated. Our world is complicated. Doubts are complicated. Often, easy answers are just too easy to be helpful because they fail to grapple with the question on its own terms.

For example, consider a student who approaches her small group leader with questions about how we know God created us. What if we are just a happy accident? A wise youth worker will not look down on this question as either predictable or the result of a liberal agenda. A one-sentence reply will rarely help. Silence is better than an easy answer, since simple answers to genuine questions can teach students to turn off their brain and decide there are no good answers. Usually, the best response is to genuinely listen, repeat back the question in your own words, and then ask a follow-up question about their question. Students will lean into honest conversations about faith and doubt when they know they'll be listened to and taken seriously.

Our answers need to reflect the reality of sin, the brokenness it has caused, and the source of our hope. Hard questions demand a kind of honesty that is rare because they grapple with the legitimate challenge behind the question. We should aim for clarity while refusing to oversimplify things in order to make the faith easier to believe.

One of the most important things a youth ministry can do is create a culture where students' doubts and questions are met with patience and grace. At the very least, doubting students are thinking about what they believe and what they don't—and that's good.   Students who never doubt or ask hard questions tend to build their faith on shallow foundations that get swept away when the storms of life strike. But those who have wrestled through doubt have dug a deeper foundation.

You Don't Need to Doubt Everything

When students are facing doubt, many of them have the impression that they need to doubt everything in order to doubt anything. But that's simply not true. For instance, it is entirely possible to doubt the virgin birth while still believing that God exists. Questioning one area of faith doesn't require skepticism everywhere.

In your ministry to students, help them identify this tension. Faith and doubt can coexist in ways that eventually make faith stronger. This is why it is important to help students identify which doubts are smokescreens for something else (like questioning the Bible's reliability because you want to sleep with your girlfriend without feeling guilty) and which doubts are genuine questions to explore. This will also let you help students hold onto foundational truths they still believe while you patiently guide them through their unresolved questions.

We Doubt from Faith

Doubting *from* faith is a funny-sounding concept, but it echoes "I believe, help my unbelief." It means we stand upon those beliefs we are already convinced of, and from that platform of faith we lean into our doubts and questions.

Everyone does this. Atheists doubt God's existence based on their faith in science. Universalists doubt God will judge unbelievers because of their faith in God's love and human goodness. We all stand upon a set of convictions that shape the way we evaluate our doubts. Help students recognize this, and encourage them to remember they don't need to throw all their Christian beliefs in the dumpster in order to doubt a few things.

Building on what we discussed in the previous chapter, what students believe about the Bible shapes the way they approach doubt. Additionally, a ministry where the gospel is known and loved becomes a safe place to wrestle with doubt, because students know that Jesus is kind even to those whose faith is still halting (Mark 9). Saving faith doesn't require perfect faith. Imperfect faith (even the size of a mustard seed) that is placed in Jesus Christ is able to save because it is not the quality of our faith, but the God in whom we have placed it.

Finally, be patient with those who doubt, just as God has been patient with you. Care for them, listen to them, and give them space to wrestle while being committed to speaking the truth to them.

MINISTERING TO STUDENTS WHO DOUBT

- Listen with patience. Be slow to give answers, because students will often feel unheard when they take the risk to ask a question that's plagued them for weeks only to have a youth worker give an immediate answer.
- Ask good questions to get to the source of their doubts.
- Repeat their questions back to them to make sure you understand their doubt. This also helps them process the discussion.
- Remember that the head and heart are connected. Even highly intellectual questions are rooted in the heart. If you only address the head, their doubts may not feel resolved.
- Highlight the objective truth of the life, death, and resurrection of Jesus Christ. If this is true, it gives confidence in God to uphold other areas of faith that may be difficult to understand and accept.

5

How Can a Loving God
Send Anyone to Hell?

Today's teenagers have been so shaped by tolerance that it's difficult for them to reconcile the love of God with his wrath. As intimidating as it is to discuss hell and eternal judgment with students, this is a significant opportunity to help them wrestle with difficult teachings of Scripture as they learn how to think Christianly. The Bible's teaching on hell is not a message of God's hatred for sinners, but displays the holiness of God in correcting injustice and evil. As challenging as these conversations are, they usually take place because something meaningful is happening in a student's life. (Note: If a student is asking about hell and judgment because they are grieving the death of a friend or family member, pastoral wisdom indicates that is a time to highlight the mercy and comfort of God for those who mourn.)

Gospel-centered youth workers highlight the grace of God in all things, and yet we must be faithful to teach all of Scripture—even judgment and wrath. Previous generations of "turn or burn" evangelistic messages have produced a generation of youth workers who rarely warn students about the very real judgment the Bible portrays. It is common to hear Christians admit they believe in hell because the Bible teaches about it but say they don't like it and wish it didn't exist. This type of thinking suggests we believe ourselves to be better judges than God—we simply don't have the power to correct him. Such thinking shows we have a weak understanding of why hell and final judgment exist. It's important for students to understand what the Bible teaches about God's judgment in both salvation and damnation.

THE BIBLE'S TEACHING ABOUT JUDGMENT AND HELL

God is perfectly holy (Exodus 3:4–6; 1 John 1:5). He is also the Creator (Genesis 1; Psalm 65). Therefore, all judgment belongs to God. People are not free to instruct God about the moral laws of the universe. This is clearly taught throughout Scripture (Job 38–41; Jeremiah 18:1–10). Jesus taught there would be a day of judgment for the righteous and the unrighteous (Matthew 25:31–46; Luke 16:19–31). This judgment will be eternal and real, reserved for both angels and humans who have sinned against God's perfect holiness (Revelation 20).

Although people often say that hell is eternal separation from God, this is not true. Whereas God's anger and judgment against sin is currently being restrained by his common grace toward all people, hell is the experience of God's unrestrained response to sin. Jesus frequently taught about hell and the judgment of God, usually in parables. Based upon Jesus's own teachings, we know that hell will be eternal (Luke 16:26) and conscious (Matthew 13:42). Denying the existence of hell requires a denial of the very words of Jesus.

Two key teachings stand out as essential for students. First, sin is human rebellion against the holiness of God. The Bible talks about sins and transgressions. *Sin* is an archery term that means "to miss the mark" and reflects failure to meet God's holy standard of righteousness (Romans 3:23). *Transgression* means a willful breaking of God's laws (Romans 4:15). When students are honest, they will confess they are guilty of both. This is no small guilt, but shows a desire to sit on God's throne as the one who determines right and wrong in our own lives.

Second, wrath is God's holy response to sin. How else should God respond to sinful rebels who have brought so much death and destruction into God's good creation? His wrath is never unfair or uncontrolled like ours can be, nor is it in opposition to his holiness or his love. It is a direct expression of his holy love against the injustices in this world that sinful men and women have introduced. God's wrath and judgment are the purifying fire that fertilizes the garden of Eden to be reborn in the new heaven and the new earth. If God did not judge sin, injustice would continue and the curse of sin (death) would never end.

Youth workers do not preach judgment in order to scare teenagers to Jesus, but to warn them of God's wrath against sin. This presents a full picture of the beautiful work Christ has done by absorbing their deserved penalty. Yes, hell is a serious and weighty topic, but it gives the good news of Jesus the fullest opportunity to shine like a diamond against the darkness.

WHY HELL IS AN ESSENTIAL ELEMENT OF CHRISTIAN FAITH

The gospel is the good news that God saves sinners by his grace through Jesus Christ. This means there is something from which we need to be saved. If there is no judgment for sin, then there is no need for salvation. Even further, Jesus's suffering and death on a cross would be a foolish sacrifice, since we were never in danger to begin with.

Some might wonder why God cannot simply forgive sin without any judgment. After all, can't God do what he wants? The following three points are not exhaustive, but provide youth workers with a basic framework to help students understand why hell and the final judgment are essential Christian doctrines.

1. **The nature of sin: rebellion against God's holiness.** Most youth workers have heard students defend their perceived self-righteousness by saying, "I haven't killed anyone and I've never been arrested. Sure, I'm not perfect. But I'm a good person." This objection, however, misunderstands how sin is measured. The penalty of sin is not determined

merely by the sin's severity, but by the one against whom the sin is committed. All sin merits an eternal judgment because it is committed against the holy and eternal God (in addition to the people who were sinned against). And sin is not just individual wrong acts—it's going away from God and going our own way, wanting to be god of our own life. Isaiah described the human condition like this, "all we like sheep have gone astray; we have turned—everyone—to his own way" (Isaiah 53:6). Our actions are wrong because our direction is wrong. God would not be holy if he simply overlooked sin. A judge who does not uphold the law would be considered unjust and would be removed. Judgment is God's proper response to sin—because sin always brings death and destruction.

2. **The character of God: the Judge.** The Bible connects God's work of creation with his right to judge: "But who are you, O man, to answer back to God? Will what is molded say to its molder, 'Why have you made me like this?'" (Romans 9:20). This right to judge is because "all things were created through him and for him" (Colossians 1:16). Quoting Scripture in response to these questions is not avoiding their complexity, but recognizes there is an element of faith involved. If students believe the Bible truly reveals to us who God is and what he is like, then it is necessary to recognize God's judgment of sin and evil.

3. **The answer to the problem of evil: justice satisfied.** Anyone who asks, "Does God care about suffering in this world?" should find comfort in the final judgment and reality of hell. God cares so much about justice that he will indeed avenge those who have been wronged, oppressed, and victimized. Those who live in relative comfort struggle with this harsh reality, but cultures where systemic oppression runs rampant will frequently cry out for judgment against those who harm them—and this is not wrong. The cries of the martyrs in Revelation 6:10 plead for the Lord's justice against their murderers. In fact, one reason why injustice continues in

the world is God's patience. Because the proper response to injustice is judgment against sinners, the Lord's gracious patience continues to invite sinners to repent and receive grace before the day of judgment comes. In this way, hell and judgment provide a surprising resolution to one of the most common reasons people lose faith. The return of Jesus Christ will bring sin and suffering to an end because his judgment against the devil and all his works will be final, and his people will experience the fulfillment of every divine promise.

6

Why Did Jesus Need to Die?

C hristianity does not merely attempt to give individuals inner peace or happiness. It declares from the rooftop that God is for us, and "if God is for us, who can be against us?" (Romans 8:31). This isn't some trite wish-dream, but is anchored firmly in the cross. The death and resurrection of Jesus Christ is at the very heart of Christianity. *Penal substitutionary atonement* is a funny-sounding term, but each word helps explain why we love the cross.

A Display of God's Justice and Grace

Penal is a strange word that has to do with the court of law. It's where we get the common word *penalty*—the negative consequence someone receives after breaking a law. By referring to Jesus's work on the cross as penal substitutionary atonement, we are recognizing that an offense has been committed that requires a penalty.

My friend Kevin Yi helps his students understand the weightiness of their sin this way: consider the difference between drawing a mustache on a poster at your local grocery store (which would be wrong, but hardly something to be arrested over) and drawing a mustache on the *Mona Lisa*. You did the same thing in each instance, but who or what you do it against makes all the difference. In the same way, even our "little sins" against a holy God have rightfully earned his eternal wrath. And yet, rather than pouring out his wrath upon all humanity, God spoke a word of grace to sinners who come in faith to Jesus.

What happened on the cross was a display of God's justice and his grace. It was an expression of justice because God dealt with sin head-on rather than brushing it aside. The gravity of the cross reflects the seriousness of sin, which we too easily overlook. If God didn't judge sin, all the injustices and evil of this world would never receive their due. So God's judgment and wrath fulfill the cry of sufferers who yearn to see their oppressors brought to justice.

And yet, in God's justice we also see his perfect grace shining in full brilliance. For "while we were still sinners, Christ died for us" (Romans 5:8). Jesus did not die on the cross because God painted himself into a corner, but out of the same joyful love that propels parents to sacrifice for their children (Hebrews 12:1–2). If students ever doubt the love or grace of God, invite them to look to Jesus and behold the cross.

THE BELIEVER'S SUBSTITUTE

When Jesus hung on the cross, he was the Christian's substitute. He took the wrath of God and died so that Christians would be set free as beloved children of God. For this to happen, he met two criteria: he was human (or he could not stand in our place) and he was holy (or he would be deserving of judgment himself and, again, could not take our place). Theologians sometimes refer to Jesus as the God-man. This isn't because Jesus is half god and half man, like Hercules. Instead, it's because Jesus is God in flesh: fully God and fully human.

Because Jesus is fully God and fully human, he is a "second Adam" who was born without a sinful nature. He had the authority to forgive sin (Matthew 9:5–8), to work miracles (Matthew 12:25–29), and to give life (Mark 5:38–42). He was the substitute for sinful believers on the cross, bearing the wrath and judgment that was ours, in order that his righteousness and holiness would become ours (Romans 5:6–8; Hebrews 2:9).

ATONEMENT

Atonement has to do with a sacrifice that satisfies a judgment or penalty against someone who is guilty. Worship and grace in the Old Testament were centered around the sacrificial system, which instructed faithful Jews to bring certain offerings to the temple as a sacrifice to atone for their sins. An animal offered as an atoning sacrifice was a type of substitute for the person making the sacrifice. Blood was spilled to express the judgment and wrath that should be upon the head of the person bringing the offering but instead fell upon the sacrificial animal. In this way, the substitutionary death atoned for the sin of the worshiper.

When Jesus came onto the scene, John the Baptist called him, "the Lamb of God, who takes away the sin of the world" (John 1:29). The sacrificial system was built as a shadow of the true substitutionary sacrifice: Jesus Christ, the Lamb of God. Jesus is the sacrificial lamb whose blood was spilled to make atonement for others. Rather than offering a sacrifice that would need to be repeated, Jesus's death was sufficient to atone for the sins of all those who believe—once and for all (1 Peter 3:18; Hebrews 10:1–18).

THE CENTRALITY OF THE CROSS

An explanation of *penal substitutionary atonement* can help students understand both why the cross was necessary and what God accomplished through it. The cross lies at the heart of the gospel because it is where the holy love of God is most clearly displayed. Without the cross, there are only more commandments to fulfill, and to break, and to atone for. But thanks be to Jesus, who perfectly kept the commandments and gives us his righteousness while taking away our sin.

7

How Do We Know Jesus Rose from the Grave?

W hat would happen if we found out Jesus never rose from the grave? As students wrestle with their faith, this is a natural question for them to ask. And it is a welcome one, since the gospel means we offer people help not only in their joyful seasons but especially in their darkest, questioning ones. How do we really know that Jesus rose from the grave? And if he didn't, how much of a difference does that make?

Paul's words in 1 Corinthians 15:17 are crucial: "If Christ has not been raised, your faith is futile and you are still in your sins." Furthermore, our hope is in the risen Christ, not merely in a set of philosophical truths: "He who raised Christ Jesus from the dead will also give life to your mortal bodies" (Romans 8:11). So, how can we help our students grow in confidence that the resurrection really happened?

This is a hinge on which all Christianity swings. If Jesus has not risen from the grave, we are wasting our time. But if he has, that changes everything. This is the primary truth students and youth leaders must return to over and over. The following proofs of the resurrection can help strengthen students' confidence in the new life of the gospel.

Eyewitnesses. The New Testament writers claimed they saw Jesus. This was unexpected and surprising, to the point that the disciples did not even believe it when they were first told (Luke 24:11, 38–43; John 20:19–29). Those who say the apostles stole the body of Jesus out of the tomb forget that Roman guards were stationed to seal and protect the tomb—and if they allowed bandits to raid the tomb, it would cost them their lives. The guards were indeed bribed, but not by the apostles. The bribe came from the chief priests who had the money and political authority to protect the guards in exchange for their silence. More than that, the disciples go so far as to say that Jesus's resurrection was physical and bodily, not just spiritual. Jesus's wounds were visible and touchable, and the closing chapters of both Luke and John contain accounts of eating with Jesus that reinforce this glorious hope. It is also notable that the first people to see the risen Christ were women. This detail is significant because women weren't highly regarded and could not provide legal testimony in court. If Jesus's resurrection had been a fabricated story, only a fool would make women the witnesses. The prominence of the women in this account can only be explained by its historical accuracy.

The date of early New Testament documents. Many of the original readers of the New Testament Gospels and letters were also eyewitnesses if they had traveled to Jerusalem for Passover the year Jesus rose. While writing about the truth of the resurrection, Paul wrote, "He appeared to Cephas, then to the twelve. Then he appeared to more than five hundred brothers at one time, most of whom are still alive, though some have fallen asleep" (1 Corinthians 15:5–6). Paul essentially says, "If you don't believe Jesus rose from the dead, go talk to some of the other people who all saw him—they're still alive."

Non-Christian writers. The life, death, and resurrection of Jesus Christ is mentioned by multiple non-Christian writers in the ancient world. Of course, they did not believe he actually rose from the grave, but they remarked about the apostles' claim that he did.[2] This is historic evidence that something significant happened in Jerusalem leading to a movement of people who were convinced Jesus was the Messiah who rose from the dead, ascended into heaven, and will come again as Judge and Savior.

A drastic change in the disciples. The Gospels routinely share instances where Jesus corrects his disciples for having little faith. When Jesus was arrested, they all deserted him and ran for their lives. Then, suddenly, they were on the streets during the festival of Pentecost preaching the gospel and declaring the resurrection of Jesus. From that day on, they endured intense opposition and persecution without wavering. If they had agreed to lie about the resurrection, what are the chances they would all endure persecution unto death over something they knew was not true? Many were killed for proclaiming the resurrection. Surely something happened to bring about such radical change. Jesus's bodily resurrection was the historic claim that launched the worldwide church. Given all the evidence, it is entirely reasonable for students to place their faith in Jesus Christ as the risen Savior.

REAL-LIFE IMPACT OF THE RESURRECTION

- The resurrection proves Jesus is the Son of God. Everything he said about himself is true.
- When students doubt, the resurrection can bolster their faith. It's easy to doubt philosophical ideas like the existence of God and the Trinity. But the resurrection is an event that anchors Christianity in history.
- Students can live with hope even in the midst of suffering. Christians will share in Christ's victory over sin and death. Youth workers can encourage students with the reminder that there is always a reason for hope: Jesus has defeated our greatest enemy.
- When students grieve the death or sickness of a friend or family member, they will experience grief but need not grieve as those who have no hope (1 Thessalonians 4:13). Instead, they can believe the gospel that death is the transition from this life into the very presence of God, where believers experience the blessing of God until its fulfillment in the new heaven and new earth.

8

Will Jesus Really Return?

Pastors often give two main reasons for rarely teaching about the end times: there are so many views it's hard to speak without feeling pressure to give every perspective equal time, and it sometimes leads to obsession among those who believe Jesus's return is only days away. These are good to keep in mind while teaching about end times, but the return of Christ is at the heart of our gospel hope. When students' earthly hopes are crushed, or in seasons of suffering, pointing them to God's eternal promise of glory is the best news we can offer. It is a great comfort to remind students that "the sufferings of this present time are not worth comparing with the glory that is to be revealed to us" (Romans 8:18).

WHY CHRIST'S RETURN IS ESSENTIAL

The Bible clearly teaches Christ will indeed come again (Acts 1:11; James 5:8, for example). If that's not going to happen, it means Jesus's understanding of his mission was faulty and unreliable—and unfinished. Salvation currently is secure but incomplete. Jesus has defeated sin and death, but his return to claim that victory will put an eternal end to their very existence.

Christian hope longs for the day when our faith will become sight and when all of God's promises receive the glorious fulfillment. Without the return of Jesus, Christians continue to live in a world marred by sin, with daily temptations to break God's law. Although death's sting is no longer lethal, it still produces intense grief and sorrow in this life. But when Jesus ushers in the new heaven and new earth described in Revelation 21 and 22, we will live in an even greater Eden where the potential for sin will have been eliminated. This is why his return is worthy of being shouted from the rooftops—not because it is a fear-inducing evangelism tactic, but because it fills us with confidence that God's promise of salvation outshines all of our expectations.

WHAT ALL CHRISTIANS BELIEVE ABOUT CHRIST'S RETURN

Despite the differences between various end-times views, there are certain truths we must affirm to remain biblically orthodox. Although students will likely be drawn to exploring the differences, it is important to highlight the shared convictions that bind Christians together as we prayerfully anticipate Christ's return.

Visibility. Acts 1:11 explicitly says, "This Jesus, who was taken up from you into heaven, will come in the same way as you saw him go into heaven." As with the resurrection, there are some who try to say Christ's return will be spiritual, not physical. But the promised new heaven and new earth will be real, and Jesus's return will also be real and visible for all to behold.

Judgment. Jesus will return as the Judge. All the sin and evil and injustice that has been perpetrated on earth will receive its rightful judgment. Those who question, "Why doesn't God stop all this suffering and evil?" will discover that he was not turning a blind eye after all, but patiently giving sinners time to repent. All who have placed their faith in Jesus Christ for salvation will be declared innocent children of God who receive eternal life. Those not in Christ will receive judgment as sinners unto eternal damnation (Revelation 20:11–15). Students benefit from clear instruction about God's judgment—not to scare them into faith, but to warn them about the terrible consequences of sin and to display for them the beauty of our salvation through Christ.

Salvation. Teaching about judgment and salvation go hand-in-hand. Without hearing about sin and judgment, there is no need for salvation in the first place. The gospel proclaims God's victory over sin and death through the cross and empty tomb. We usually stop there, but we should also proclaim that in the new heaven and new earth God will finish what he started.

Kingdom. Many students are astounded when they hear that we will have real, physical bodies in the new heaven and new earth. Too often, the kingdom of God is taught in ways that are so abstract and spiritual there is no real consideration for the biblical language of Isaiah 65 and Revelation 21, which describe a renewed earth that is also the heavenly place of God, since he has come to live with his people. When Jesus returns as Judge and Savior, all creation will rejoice in salvation's fulfillment. Sin and death will have no place, for the kingdom of God will be fully realized and God's children will enjoy it for all eternity. This is good news indeed.

MAKING SENSE OF THE DIFFERENT END-TIMES VIEWS

Details surrounding the end times, like the rapture, millennium, and role of Israel, are hotly contested issues that sometimes cause division between Christians when we lose sight of the clear truths we agree on. The following is a brief summary of the four major views on end times that fall within the realm of evangelical Christianity. Although youth workers will rarely teach these views to students, it is important to have a basic understanding of them because students may hear certain teachings and look to their mentors for guidance.

Historic premillennialism. According to historic premillennialism, Jesus will return after the great tribulation to establish the millennial (thousand-year) kingdom on earth. Most historic pretribulationalists do not believe in a two-stage rapture of the church, but that believers will be raptured to meet with Christ in the clouds in order to greet him and usher him into his millennial kingdom. At this time, there will be a great influx of Jewish believers, and Christians will reign with Christ over the nations. Sin will remain, but will be kept in check by the rule of Christ. At the end of the millennium there will be a great judgment of Satan and of all those who oppose Christ while the eternal kingdom of God is fully established in the new heaven and new earth.

Dispensational premillennialism. In the dispensational view, salvation history is broken into eras (known as dispensations) in which God deals with his people in different ways. We are currently living in the sixth of seven dispensations, with the millennial kingdom yet to come. Dispensationalists believe Jesus's return will be a two-stage event: first he will return to rapture Christians (both living and dead) out of the world as a rescue from the great tribulation, and then he will return again after a seven-year tribulation to usher in the millennial kingdom. The final judgment takes place upon Jesus's full return, after the great tribulation, and will introduce the new heaven and new earth. While this view has become prevalent among Christians in North America in the past two hundred years, historic premillennialism is the most historically-attested premillennial view.

Amillennialism. This position states that the millennium is not a literal thousand years but a symbolically-long duration of time that began with Christ's resurrection or at Pentecost and will continue until Christ's return. The tribulation and millennium are commingled: Christians today are actively persecuted even as the church expands throughout the whole earth through the proclamation of the gospel. Amillennialists do not believe the Bible teaches anything about a rapture of Christians out from persecution, but that God strengthens his people to endure opposition. The final judgment will take place immediately when Jesus returns, at which time he will usher in the new heaven and new earth.

Postmillennialism. In this view, the tribulation has already taken place and the church is presently ushering in the millennium through the spread of the gospel. Sin will not cease, but it will be greatly minimized as the gospel transforms cultures. When the nations have been evangelized and the influence of the gospel has reached its peak, Jesus will return and establish the new heaven and new earth.

9
Who (Not What) Is the Holy Spirit?

The Holy Spirit is the third person of the Trinity, equal with the Father and the Son. This is why it is concerning when Christians call the Holy Spirit an "it" rather than "he." Personal pronouns exist to highlight personal agency. Students need God's personal presence, not an impersonal force.

Youth workers often feel intimidated about talking about the Holy Spirit. The Father and the Son (Jesus) are easy to discuss, but discussing the Holy Spirit seems mystical and unfamiliar. Plus, the gifts of the Spirit are controversial, so it feels safer to leave the Holy Spirit to professional theologians. And yet, the Holy Spirit is God. If Christians avoid talking about the Holy Spirit, they will have a poor understanding of the God they worship.

Discipling students to have a clear view of the Holy Spirit equips them to walk in step with the Spirit and to rely on his strength for their sanctification. This truth can give youth workers great comfort in those discouraging seasons of ministry when it seems nothing is working and students simply aren't responding. We must remember that the Holy Spirit is the one who accomplishes the work of ministry.

WHAT THE HOLY SPIRIT DOES

- **Applies salvation to the believer.** All three persons of the Trinity are involved in the work of salvation. The

Father sent the Son to make atonement for sinners, and the Spirit applies that grace to the children of God. He brings conviction of sin that leads sinners to saving faith in Christ (John 16:8), and unites them to Christ (1 John 4:13). He clothes us in the righteousness of Christ and does the inner work of sanctification (2 Thessalonians 2:13).

- **Advocates.** The Holy Spirit is sometimes called the *Paraclete*, which comes from the Greek word used in John's gospel that's translated as "Helper," "Advocate," or "Counselor." The Bible describes the Spirit's ministry not primarily as that of a counselor-therapist, but a counselor-lawyer. He even prays for us when we don't know what to say (Romans 8:26–27).

- **Teaches.** Mark 13:11 has a helpful explanation: "And when they bring you to trial and deliver you over, do not be anxious beforehand what you are to say, but say whatever is given you in that hour, for it is not you who speak, but the Holy Spirit." The Holy Spirit not only speaks for us to the Father, but also gives us the words to speak to others. Jesus promised that when he went away, "the Helper, the Holy Spirit, whom the Father will send in my name, he will teach you all things and bring to your remembrance all that I have said to you" (John 14:26). This promise was given directly to the apostles who would carry the gospel into a new world. It continues to remind Christians of the Holy Spirit's ongoing help today, as he illuminates our minds to the Word of God in Scripture. This promise also bolsters our confidence in the Scriptures as being "breathed out by God" (2 Timothy 3:16), because the authors were under the guidance of the Holy Spirit. Our confidence in teaching God's Word is bolstered by Jesus's promise that the Holy Spirit empowers the work of the Great Commission in Acts 1:8 and is displayed in Acts 4:31. The Spirit is the teacher of God's people.

- **Sanctifies.** By receiving the grace of God through Jesus Christ through the indwelling Spirit (1 Corinthians 3:16), Christians are being transformed into the image of Christ (Romans 15:16; Colossians 3:10). The Spirit applies the grace of God, leads sinners to repentance, and strengthens believers in the midst of temptation—even in ways they are likely unaware of. We read of "the fruit of the Spirit," not the fruit of our efforts, because godliness is the result of the Spirit's work rather than the Christian's hard work to produce it. Although parents and youth workers may play a pivotal role when students are swimming in a cesspool of sin, it is the Holy Spirit who will ultimately convict their hearts and transform their lives.

- **Gives gifts.** The Holy Spirit empowers God's people for ministry. The Bible's lists of spiritual gifts do not create a hierarchy of important people in the church, but rather show that all believers with all kinds of gifts contribute to building up the church. This should empower Christians to live in a way that each believer (regardless of age) plays an important role in Christ-exalting ministry among God's people and among the spiritually lost. Mature believers have a wonderful opportunity to mentor teenage Christians, equipping them to use their spiritual gifts for the glory of God. God equips those he calls, often while they are in the midst of obedience rather than before. For this reason, spiritual-gifts tests are not always helpful. Ensure that students are not hedged into their "giftedness," but freed up to serve according to the opportunities God provides.

WALKING IN STEP WITH THE SPIRIT

All Christians, regardless of their age, are called to walk in step with the Spirit (Galatians 5:16–26). This involves turning away from sin and walking in Spirit-prompted holiness. Faithful youth workers help students recognize their dependence on the

Holy Spirit rather than burdening students with pressure to produce their own sanctification. The gospel is not a message that cries out "try harder, do better," but an invitation to cease striving and receive grace Christ through faith.

In a culture that places great emphasis on dreaming big and changing the world (consider the most popular messages high school graduates hear every year), youth workers invite students to rest in Christ and walk with him. The following habits are not presented as a to-do list, but simply as practices that are common among Christians who are increasingly walking in step with the Spirit.

First, Christians rely on the Word of God. How can they rely on it if they do not read it? Teaching students how to read the Bible and equipping them to cultivate it as a lifelong practice may be the single most effective thing you can do for a new Christian. The Holy Spirit inspired Scripture, and he will continue to speak through it. By giving students the Scriptures, we are trusting the Word of God to do the work of God. Students who are walking in the Spirit walk with the Bible in their hands.

Second, students who are walking in step with the Spirit have a deepening prayer life. They do not only pray before meals or a big test, but throughout the day and during dedicated moments of intercession for others. Students who are growing in their faith will experience a deepening fellowship with God, and this happens largely through prayer.

Third, Christians transformed by the grace of Christ will have a desire for the message of the gospel to transform others. They will become evangelists. This is not a mysterious spiritual gift only a few receive, but a basic Christian conviction: "This is the greatest message in the world, I want to share it with others!" Since the Holy Spirit draws the lost to Christ, it only makes sense that walking with the Spirit deepens students' evangelistic zeal.

Fourth, they want to be with the people of God. Being at church and youth group will not be measured by how entertaining and fun it is, but will become a sweet experience because there is a growing sense of, "These are my people. I belong here."

Finally, they will receive correction from parents, youth workers, and other authority figures with humility.

In all these ways, students who are growing in their faith will be increasingly different from their non-Christian peers. They will live with an abiding awareness that they are dependent on the strength of the Holy Spirit. Walking in step with the Spirit is not for super-powered Christians but for everyone—teenagers included—whose lives demonstrate the faithfulness of God to save sinners.

10
Why Is the Church Important?

Youth workers often hear the common statistics about the church dropout rate: two-thirds of teenagers who were active in youth ministry stop attending church between the ages of 18–22.³ Although some details in these studies might make the results less alarming, the big idea stands: teenagers are leaving the church, and most of them are not returning (even after they start a family). But one common trait of students who remain in the church throughout adolescence and into adulthood is a sense of belonging in the local church. To these students, church is not simply where youth group takes place; it is a family of worshipers where they belong.

It should be the normal pattern of ministry to students that they worship with other believers of all ages. The biblical words *church* and *synagogue* mean "gathering" or "assembly." If students are not worshiping with the gathered body of believers, they might attend youth group but they do not attend church. Is it any wonder, then, that they continue to not attend church after they graduate?

WHY TEENAGERS BELONG IN THE CHURCH

When students turn from sin and confess faith in Jesus Christ, the Holy Spirit unites them with Christ and they become members of the body of Christ, the *universal church* (Ephesians 1:22–23). As members of this universal church, they are spiritually adopted into a family of faith that includes Christians from all languages, ethnicities, and periods of history. For example, Christian teenagers in rural Texas are one in Christ with persecuted Christians in Iran. This means Christians are members of the most diverse, multiethnic, and persecuted group of people in the world today. The implications are enormous—including how we teach students to spend their money, intercede for others in prayer, combat racism, and think about global politics.

The *local church* is a particular expression of the universal church. It would have been unthinkable for first-century Christians to have the freedom Western teenagers enjoy and yet prefer worshiping privately at home rather than with the body of Christ. As God's people come together for worship, God is glorified. Youth ministry is not a church, but a ministry of the church whose mission is to make disciples of the next generation. Integrating students into the local church is not only the most effective way to ensure students will continue in their faith, it is simply biblical. Teenage Christians are not merely children in the church, but spiritual brothers and sisters in the faith—and they should be treated as such by the church leaders and members.

Gathering with God's people for worship, prayer, and to hear the Scriptures preached is a means of grace that nourishes students' minds and hearts. Even if they are blind to it as it is happening, worship is formative and provides students with great comfort when their life plans crumble. Often, the songs they sang and the Bible verses they learned while growing are how the Lord applies the gospel to their hearts when they find themselves wallowing in mud like the Prodigal Son.

Sanctification doesn't happen in solitary confinement. The first thing that God said was not good was for Adam to be alone, because people were created for community. Spiritual maturity is rarely found in isolated Christians, but is found in increasing measure among those who provide fellowship and support for others. Students also receive mentoring and find godly role models when they get to know other adults in the church—but this will be impossible if students are not meaningfully engaged in the life of the church, but are only with fellow teenagers.

Ministry to others is a significant component of a student's spiritual development. Attending programs without any meaningful involvement turns students into spiritual consumers who stand on the sidelines and evaluate whether or not the program is meeting their needs. Pastors are called to "equip the saints for the work of ministry" (Ephesians 4:12). This includes teenage Christians, and it simply will not bear long-term fruit unless it includes involvement in the life of the whole church. Empowering students with responsibilities that matter can be risky, but it is an extremely effective discipleship opportunity that also proves you mean it when you tell them, "You belong here. You matter. We want you engaged in the ministry."

Participation in the body of Christ gives students a preview of what godliness looks like in various life-stages: as newlyweds, as parents, when your wife has cancer, when your kids have abandoned the faith, as a widow, or as a fifty-year-old who has never married. These are important people for students to learn from and know. As families become increasingly fragmented, this is one of the greatest treasures the local church can provide.

Practical Ways to Foster Student Belonging

- Worship together with all generations as often as reasonably possible. If your services are entirely separate now, propose a quarterly shared worship service to introduce the vision to the congregation.
- Encourage students to serve in the kids' ministry. This is often the most accessible place for younger teenagers to begin serving, and pairing them with a lead teacher provides them with a mentor.
- Plug students into existing ministries like worship team, media ministry, or hospitality. Students have

gifts and passions that enable them to offer meaningful contributions while learning from other members of the church.

- Participate in events that aren't youth-specific. If your church is hosting an event, don't always assume it's lame. Ask if it would be appropriate to invite students to participate, and encourage parents to bring the whole family. Only inviting students to youth-ministry events sends the wrong message to both students and older members of the church.

- Remind teenagers that many adults are intimidated by groups of teenagers, especially when they seem closed-off from interacting with the rest of the church. Encourage students to adopt a posture that invites older members to engage them in conversation. If the students are tired of being treated like immature kids, call them to demonstrate maturity and to initiate simple and kind conversations with adults.

- Create informal opportunities outside of normal church activities where the generations can interact and learn about each other. Picnics, cookouts, days at the beach, and other informal gatherings are incredibly fruitful ways for children and teenagers to see the adults in the church in a completely new light.

- Invite leaders in the church to visit youth group to share their testimonies. Be sure, however, that these men and women do not simply arrive just before they give their talk and leave right after. Encourage them to be fully invested in the night, as much as they are able. This will help break down walls and foster approachability.

11

How Do Christians Interpret the Old Testament?

When you look at your Bible, you'll notice only one binding. One book, all Scripture. As 1 Timothy 3:16–17 famously declares, "All Scripture is breathed out by God and profitable for teaching, for reproof, for correction, and for training in righteousness, that the man of God may be competent, equipped for every good work." It's important to remember that the Scripture being referred to is what we call the Old Testament.

The Bible is one book, composed of both the Old and New Testaments, equally inspired and authoritative for Christians. And yet, most Christians have no guilt over enjoying a delicious lobster even though shellfish is forbidden by Mosaic law. This raises an important question: How should Christians interpret the Old Testament in light of the New, and how does this affect student ministry?

SALVATION HISTORY

Christians cannot rightly understand and interpret the Old Testament without a proper understanding of salvation history—the whole-Bible story of how God saves his people. To review, this one story has four chapters:

1. **Creation: Know where we come from.** God made everything, and it was good, perfect, and holy. People were created in the image of God to worship and serve him as his representatives on earth.

2. **Fall: Know our need.** When Adam and Eve sinned, death spread throughout all of creation. God's image in people remains, but it is fallen and shattered like a broken mirror that still reflects but with varying degrees of accuracy. All creation groans for redemption.

3. **Redemption: Know how God meets our need.** Time and again throughout Israel's history, God sent saviors, performed saving acts, and established rituals to prepare his people for the coming Savior. Many of these served as figures or "types" that pointed to the one true Savior who would bring redemption. At the right time, Jesus Christ came, lived, and died as the atoning sacrifice for our sin. Through faith in Jesus, we receive new hearts and are adopted as sons and daughters of God. We are united with Christ by the indwelling Holy Spirit who sanctifies and strengthens us in faith and godliness. The New Testament proclaims this gospel and then applies it to show what a godly life looks like.

4. **Consummation: Know where we are headed.** We live in confident expectation that the promise of the new heaven and new earth will not simply restore the garden of Eden, but surpass it (see the description in Revelation 21 and 22). No longer will sin or temptation have any ability to bring about civil war in creation— sin and death will be utterly defeated. This means the fruit of sin is eternally gone. No more death or sorrow or injustice or pain. Everything that has become corrupted and broken will be more than restored; it will be glorified. God's kingdom will be fully consummated and we will live without guilt or shame in the presence of God.

Youth workers should model for students how to read the Bible in context, keeping in mind a broad view of the whole-Bible story no matter which part of the story a particular passage is telling.

TYPES OF OLD TESTAMENT LAWS

Understanding that not all Old Testament laws are the same is extremely important. It explains why Christians quote Scripture to say homosexuality is sinful but say eating bacon is delicious. The Old Testament laws have traditionally been broken into three categories, each with different implications for the Christian today.

- **Moral law.** These are laws that go back to what it means to be created in the image of God. They need to be obeyed and upheld by all people everywhere. This most notably includes the Ten Commandments, all of which are anchored in creation rather than in the formation of Israel. These laws include such moral principles as the hideousness of idolatry, the value of human life, the sacredness of marriage, and the importance of telling the truth.
- **Civil law.** Israel received a set of laws that specifically applied to their nation. Therefore, since you do not live in ancient Israel, these laws do not directly apply to you today. These laws included legal codes and duties such as welcoming foreigners. From them, Christians learn basic principles about what creates a good society and how the Lord wants us to treat others. But they are no longer binding in the same way they were for Ancient Israel.
- **Ceremonial law.** Ceremonial laws pertained to the temple, priests, sacrifices, and other aspects of Old Testament worship and cleanliness. Many of these laws overlap with civil law (for example, the dietary code) because Israel's spiritual and civil life were deeply

integrated. These laws show us the holiness and purity God requires for acceptable worship, and they reflect God's provision of grace for those who looked forward to the coming Messiah. Because Jesus is the Lamb of God and our Great High Priest, he is the fulfillment and end of the ceremonial law. We no longer keep it.

USE OF THE LAW FOR CHRISTIANS TODAY

Another helpful distinction is the difference between law and gospel. God's moral law tells you what you're supposed to do, but the gospel tells you what God has done or has promised to do. This distinction helps us understand three primary purposes of God's law:

1. **The law mirrors.** When we look into God's law, we come face to face with the reality that we are sinners (Romans 7:7). The law cannot rescue us from sin any more than a mirror can wash a dirty face. But without the law, we simply wouldn't realize our need for ongoing confession, repentance, and grace. So the law shows us our need for the gospel, prompting us to turn to Jesus daily.

2. **The law curbs.** The law curbs public chaos and preserves social order. God's law promotes what is good for humanity and for creation. Without law, we would live in anarchy. In this sense, whether someone is a Christian or not, they benefit from God's law because it preserves creation's innate order.

3. **The law guides.** The law also serves as a guide in our holiness. We rely on the commands of God to know what we are progressing toward in sanctification. If we want to know what God expects of us, we should read the law—not only in the Old Testament, but also the commands of the New Testament. It is important to remember that "the law is good if one uses it properly" (1 Timothy 1:8 NIV); that is, if one uses the law as a guide

to holiness while relying on the indwelling Holy Spirit for the power to do what the law commands.

This discussion surrounding God's law highlight's the perfect righteousness of Jesus. He perfectly kept every commandment, and we are clothed in his active righteousness by faith. In this way, Christians are indeed saved by law-keeping—but not our own. Youth workers help students recognize the good and proper use of the law is to lead them to Jesus.

Discipling students into lifelong faith requires youth workers to equip them to read and understand the Bible. Without modeling and teaching faithful biblical theology, students may consider the New Testament to be the Word of God while treating the Old Testament as merely background information. Remember, the Old Testament was Jesus's Bible, it was the Bible of the apostles, and it remains God-breathed Scripture. Read it with confidence, but also with wisdom. Since we are not Israel, not everything is applied as directly as it might seem. Read and teach God's laws and promises in light of those to whom they were given and what their function was meant to be. Whether the laws apply directly to students today or not, they remain worthy of our study and attention, for they tell us something about the heart and character of our God who saves.

12

Can Christians Believe in Evolution?

M any teenagers live with the assumption that science and faith cannot coexist. Often, this is reinforced by youth groups that either completely avoid conversations about creation and evolution or discuss it in a way that dismisses scientific claims as a purely atheistic agenda. But youth workers can have fruitful conversations with students about the claims of science and especially evolution. It helps to consider the glory of creation and the complexity of understanding how God created it, while holding some convictions about science.

First, science is good. Sadly, the stereotype of religious folk is that we are unscientific, or even anti-science. And yet, most of Western history's greatest scientists were faithful Christians who practiced science as a way to explore God's good creation—consider Johannes Kepler, Galileo, Francis Bacon, and Isaac Newton, to name only a few. Today, however, many people have replaced faith in God with naturalism, which says, "If I can't physically and scientifically prove it, then it isn't real." That naturalistic worldview has no place among those who profess to worship Jesus, but Christians are not opposed to science. Youth workers are wise to encourage students to frame their scientific studies as an exploration of the incredible world God created.

Second, research leads to multiple interpretations. There isn't always one clear and obvious conclusion to scientific inquiries, and scientists often draw different interpretations from the same information. The popular voice isn't always correct. Without room to debate interpretations, the best-funded voice that affirms what people want to believe will often prevail. Scientific research and debate are good on every level, and it is good for Christians to participate in genuine scientific inquiry.

Third, science is limited to exploring fields of research within its own bounds. This means science cannot fully know something beyond the natural world. This is a built-in limitation naturalism needs to acknowledge. Expecting science to reveal something beyond the limits of science is irrational.

Fourth, even the most literal creationist agrees there is some adaptation within species. Adaptation and evolution *within* species make clear scientific sense to everyone. For example, dogs with thick fur will endure colder climates than shorthaired breeds.[4] The evolution debate revolves around whether or not one species can evolve into a new species, not whether or not one species can adapt and evolve.

SUMMARY OF POPULAR VIEWS ABOUT CREATION

1. **Young-earth creation:** God created the earth in six 24-hour days. Genesis 1 and 2 use the word "day" to mean a 24-hour day and should be taken at face value. The earth is thousands (not millions or billions) of years old. Adam and Eve were historical people whom God specially made in his image, and who sinned and were then sent out of the garden.

2. **Old-earth creation:** God created the earth, but not in 24-hour days. Genesis 1 and 2 describe what God did but not precisely how he did it, so there's some room for science to fill in the details God left out of the biblical account. The earth is probably very old, but Adam and Eve were

historical people whom God specially made in his image, and who sinned and were then sent out of the garden.

3. **Framework hypothesis:** Genesis 1 is not an account intending to tell *how* God created the world (in what order or how long he took), but a poetic way to teach *why*. This view highlights that the Bible's creation account is laid out to teach us that a Creator King built a kingdom, populated it, and placed men and women to rule over it.[5] With this interpretation there is much room for scientific explanations of how God did this. Most framework proponents view Genesis 2 as historical, meaning Adam and Eve were historical people who were specially and distinctly created by God in his image, and who sinned and were then sent out of the garden.

4. **Theistic evolution:** God initiated and used evolution to create humanity. Theistic evolution can encompass a wide range of views, all generally holding to some form of old-earth creation, with some going so far as to claim God didn't personally oversee the evolutionary process but merely set it up to happen naturally. Typically, Adam and Eve are not viewed as historic people. Instead, they are symbolic figures who describe humanity's sinful condition and rebellion against God. (Theistic evolution is a broad camp, so these descriptions may not apply to all its adherents.)

WHAT CHRISTIANS MUST AFFIRM ABOUT CREATION

In all these discussions about creation and evolution, it's tempting to be overwhelmed and shout with exasperation, "Why does this matter? I give up!" Youth workers don't need to know every answer. But regardless of particular convictions, there are some non-negotiables to emphasize to students.

God created. "In the beginning, God created the heavens and the earth" (Genesis 1:1). However creation happened, it is because God caused it. The creation of the world took place by the personal will and love of God. Because God created the world, he is worthy of worship. We lead students to Jesus, the incarnate Word who spoke creation into existence (John 1:1–14). Their Savior is also the giver of life.

God created man and woman in his image. "So God created man in his own image, in the image of God he created him; male and female he created them" (Genesis 1:27). Humanity is not a happy accident. Instead, we are special among all creation because God specifically set us apart to reflect his glory on the earth. Because we share the image of God, we represent him. We are not here for our own glory, to create monuments to ourselves, or to take advantage of others and the earth God created. Instead we are placed here to love God and love people. This includes cultivating, caring for, and building on the earth for God's glory and the good of all. God is the Creator, and so we create. God is the giver of life, and so we promote life. God is the Savior of creation, and so we forgive and restore what has been broken. When students feel worthless and like an utter failure, they can remember in whose image they were created. Helping students understand the ways God's image has been broken within us because of sin will empower them to rightly understand their sin and to believe that the gospel is given to us so we can turn to Jesus and that his Spirit will restore the image of Christ in them (Ephesians 4:17–24).

Adam and Eve are historic people. The account of Adam and Eve is never mentioned in Scripture as anything other than historical and reliable. Even when some symbolism is referenced (Romans 5:12–18; 1 Corinthians 15:45–48), it is anchored in Adam and Eve's historic sin and its effects upon all creation. Although Adam is a symbolic figurehead for all humanity, his historicity (and that of the first sin) is crucial to salvation history—otherwise God's wrath toward his fallen creation becomes a metaphor rather than a real problem in need of a real Savior. The story of humanity flows from Adam and Eve being real, historical people whose sin and promised salvation continue to impact students' lives today.

BRINGING SCIENCE TO YOUTH MINISTRY

Most youth workers are not professional scientists. Therefore, discussing science with students can be a daunting and overwhelming task. When push comes to shove, creation and evolution are the primary topics related to science that students want to discuss. After all, if scientific naturalists are right and truth must be scientifically proven, then there cannot be any universal or inherent meaning to human life and it is up to individuals to discover their own purpose.

One of the best ways youth workers can anchor teenagers in a Christian worldview is to include guest speakers who can speak with credibility about the scientific evidence for biblical teachings. These men and women might be members of your church or a local Christian school or university. This is one of the topics where guest speakers are most effective, but be sure to find out beforehand what they believe and what they will say.

13

Should Christians Be Tolerant?

Tolerance means respect despite disagreement, and it's the new Golden Rule. Worldly tolerance preaches a gospel of unhindered self-expression, captured by the frequent saying, "You do you." Christians are often labeled as intolerant for stating their convictions and attempting to persuade others of the truth of Scripture. By this worldly definition of tolerance, the only thing that should not be tolerated is intolerance.

We may be tempted to take the all-too-common approach of pointing out the irony of intolerance against Christians who affirm historic Christian teaching. But it's far more helpful to consider how the gospel leads Christians to love their enemies and pray for those who persecute them.

When the apostles were arguing about who was the greatest, Jesus instructed them to live differently. The world seeks power through authority, but Christians are called to be servants, even as Jesus himself came "to serve, and to give his life as a ransom for many" (Matthew 20:28). Christians are called to live differently. When we debate and seek our rights the same way the world does, arguing against intolerance with a defensive spirit that asks "Why won't you be tolerant of us?" our attitude is out of line with the example of Christ.

What Tolerance Is (and Isn't)

It's common to hear advocates of worldly tolerance quote Jesus in Matthew 7:1, "Do not judge, or you too will be judged (NIV)." And they're right to do so. Quoting Jesus is always a good idea, and Christians shouldn't be known as judges who eagerly bring their verdicts upon the guilty. But this does not mean Jesus is advocating for a "live and let live" version of tolerance. Jesus continues by saying, "How can you say to your brother, 'Let me take the speck out of your eye,' when there is the log in your own eye? You hypocrite, first take the log out of your own eye, and then you will see clearly to take the speck out of your brother's eye" (vv. 4–5). Jesus's warning was against judging others while being guilty of the very same thing. His own words make it clear that all have God-given standards to meet, and once his disciples are "able to see clearly" they should help their brother remove the speck from his eye. It is also worth highlighting that Jesus is addressing how brothers—fellow Christians—judge one another. It should not be with a motive to tear down, but to strengthen. Nonbelievers are another matter: they need the gospel, not our correction.

Instead of viewing tolerance as a sinful compromise, Christians see tolerance as an expression of loving their enemies. There are many other examples available: Jesus's instruction to go the extra mile, to turn the other cheek, and to pray for those who persecute you—plus Jesus's interactions with lepers and adulterers and tax collectors. He is gracious and tolerant, but always in a way that invites others into relationship without ignoring their sin.

Yes, Jesus's kind of tolerance assumes disagreement. Otherwise, there's nothing to tolerate. Most people acknowledge this in theory, but practice tolerance as if tolerance equals agreement. Real tolerance is respect despite disagreement.

As their peers are increasingly post-Christian, it is important for Christian teenagers to assume a tolerant posture without buying into the culture's twisted definition of tolerance. This is not a passive-aggressive ceasefire: both parties involved still believe they are right and the other is wrong, and they will continue trying to persuade the other. But they do so with genuine respect and kindness. *This* is the kind of tolerance needed today. And this is a version of tolerance Christians can embrace, because it's simply an expression of loving your neighbor—and your enemy—as yourself.

RULES OF ENGAGEMENT FOR STUDENTS IN A TOLERANT AGE

- **Listen, listen, listen.** It is impossible to respect someone you won't listen to. Being a good listener, especially when talking about spiritual things, will show someone you truly value them. Good listeners want to really understand what the other person is saying. They don't merely listen in order to find holes to exploit in the other person's argument. If you are constantly thinking about what you're going to say next in order to win the debate, you aren't listening—you're plotting. Listen first.

- **Repeat back.** If you can't repeat back what the other person just said in a way that they would respond, "Yes, that's what I believe!" you are not ready to voice your disagreement. No one feels respected when someone twists their words and critiques a strawman argument. That is cheap and disrespectful. Instead, ask clarifying questions to make sure you really understand, and demonstrate your respect by repeating back what they just said before you disagree. This often changes the tone from a debate to a conversation.

- **Keep the main thing the main thing.** Jesus is the main thing. What good is it if you present irrefutable evidence about creation or traditional sexuality or whatever else you may be discussing, but the person still rejects the gospel? Those topics are important, but they are not at the heart of what it means to be a Christian. If you are more passionate about debating certain hot topics than you are about presenting the gospel, you have lost the main thing. That said, forcing Jesus into the conversation can sometimes feel like a disingenuous setup. When you are fluent in the language of the gospel and understand how it shapes all of life, you will be able to identify some regular on-ramps from which the gospel can enter your conversations. And keeping Jesus the main thing in your own heart will keep him the main thing in your conversations too—for he alone gives new life.

14

How Should Christians Think about Mental Health Struggles?

Recent statistics suggest nearly one-third of teenagers regularly struggle with anxiety and depression, while two-thirds consider it a major concern among their peers.[6] Everyone walks through sad or anxious seasons in life, but these students are experiencing something deeper and more overwhelming: a sense of despair with no hope for improvement. Some people might dismiss these facts, claiming that diagnoses are too easily given, but it's a stretch to argue there's not a problem.

Youth workers are not psychologists or trained counselors. Their central mission is to proclaim the good news of Jesus Christ to students and to mentor them into spiritual maturity. Yet many youth workers ask, "Does faith in God help students who have a mental health diagnosis?" It does!

But affirming the power of the gospel for those who suffer from mental health diagnoses does not mean youth workers should overlook the legitimate and complicated factors and treatments for students' diagnoses. With this in mind, it is helpful for youth workers to have a basic understanding of the most common mental health diagnoses and how the gospel shapes ministry to students who have received a diagnosis. This will prevent the temptation to reply flippantly to students' mental health struggles by quoting a Bible verse and saying "Have more faith and try harder."

Mental health is nothing new, even if it's a term the older generations did not use. Look no further than the Psalms: "Why, my soul, are you downcast? Why so disturbed within me?" (Psalm 43:5 NIV). Elijah was crippled by anxiety and depression when God spoke to him in a soft voice (1 Kings 19). If faith eliminated mental health struggles, there would be fewer psalms expressing how anxiety and depression can plague those who trust in God.

Some Christians wonder if it is faithless to take medication for mental health disorders. Most people know Christians who minimize the seriousness of mental health struggles by encouraging those who suffer to simply pray more. While every Christian would benefit from a more committed prayer life, this advice is often given in a dismissive manner that communicates that the friend's suffering is due to a lack of faith. But the corrective to this false view is not a wholesale embrace of all medicine as a pharmaceutical savior, either. Instead, good pastoral care comes alongside the friend with gospel-bought hope and patient friendship that flows from a robust view of sin's effects on humanity.

Mental health problems are one element of the fallenness humanity endures in this world that awaits restoration in the new heaven and new earth. Until then, Christians cling to the gospel even while they take their medicine. Medicine is a gift from God, and should be viewed as a providential means of help for those who suffer. But it should not be a Christian's first response when faced with a potential mental health diagnosis. Whether the medicine is to help them with anxiety, depression, ADHD, OCD, or some other diagnosis, their Savior's name is Jesus Christ. He is the one who brings true hope for healing and restoration, even while they take their medicine with breakfast in the morning.

COMMON MENTAL HEALTH DIAGNOSES

- **Anxiety.** Every person has experienced anxiety. Jesus directly addresses it in Matthew 6:25–34 when he repeatedly says, "Do not be anxious." Christians are called to live by faith, not in anxiety. Most people experience elevated stress, which often presents as anxiety, over particularly challenging circumstances, whether it is over a big test, conflict with friends, or tryouts for a sports team or theatrical performance. But this is not the same thing as clinical anxiety. *Generalized anxiety disorder* (GAD) includes an overwhelming feeling of dread over life in general (not over any particular event or issue) for an extended period of time. *Panic disorder* occurs when students periodically experience anxiety with physical symptoms that may feel like a heart attack—racing pulse, sweating, and chest tightening. *Social anxiety disorder* happens when students either worry about the social repercussions of their anxiety so much they avoid social interaction, or when they experience feelings similar to panic while in social situations.

- **Depression.** Similar to anxiety, depression is something many people experience for a season following something painful or difficult. When depression lasts for a prolonged period of time or leaves a student feeling like life isn't worth living anymore, it's time to consult a mental health expert. The range of symptoms for depression in teenagers can vary widely, so it's most important to look for significant behavior changes. When a teenager suddenly becomes lethargic and unmotivated, or high-strung with sudden outbursts of anger, youth workers and parents will want to pay careful attention. It is also important to notice how the student talks about himself or herself and about the value of life. Talk with the student's parents about your concerns. Especially encourage them to seek professional help if you fear a student is heading toward self-harm.

- **Eating disorders.** Eating disorders often hide beneath anxiety and depression, so it is important for youth workers to know some warning signs. *Anorexia* is a disorder in which students significantly restrict their food intake, sometimes to the point of not eating for extensive periods of time. *Bulimia* usually involves a cycle of binge eating and then purging through vomiting or use of laxatives. There are other eating disorders, too, like *orthorexia*—a disruptive obsession with healthy eating. Today's youth culture, with its obsession about appearances and the prevalence of social media, provides fertile soil for negative body image. Partner with parents in helping students develop a biblical view of the body.

APPLYING THE GOSPEL TO MENTAL HEALTH STRUGGLES

The gospel is good news that anchors the Christian in the love and grace of God. When students struggle with their mental health, youth workers should validate these struggles even while pointing students' eyes to see the cross as a clear demonstration of God's love. The battle for mental health can easily lead students to shame and insecurity, but the gospel assures students their worth and lovability is secure because of God's promise.

Faithful youth workers, especially those who have faced their own mental health struggles, can come alongside students and their parents to listen, weep, laugh, and remind them of the glorious promise we have because Jesus rose from the grave and overcame the curse of sin. The gospel gives hope for today ("God still loves me and he is with me") and hope for the future ("God will make everything right"). In John 10:10, Jesus says, "The thief comes only to steal and kill and destroy. I came that they may have life and have it abundantly."

May the next generation increasingly discover the abundant life that comes by the gracious hand of the Good Shepherd. Faith in Jesus does not promise a smooth road and to fix life's trials, but God promises his presence, love, and eternal hope because of the empty tomb. This is a message worth sharing with students.

15

Does Committing Suicide Condemn You to Hell?

I answer this question about suicide with great trepidation because of the complicated reasons why students ask it. There are pastoral concerns to consider because when students ask about suicide, it's usually for one of two reasons: they have a friend or loved one who recently committed suicide and they are grieving over that person's eternal fate, or they themselves are quietly wrestling with suicide as their own escape plan for the trials of this life. In both cases, we tenderly hold out the gospel and invite students to find hope and comfort in God's promise that because of Jesus Christ sinners can become the dearly loved children of God.

God is the author and giver of life. Death is also in God's hands. Taking a life is murder—whether it's someone else's life or one's own. It is not for men or women to decide when they are born, and neither should it be their decision when they die. Life is a gift to treasure and protect, and suicide is self-murder. With this understanding in mind, let's consider whether or not someone who committed suicide could still have been a real Christian, and whether or not suicide automatically condemns a person to hell.

THE UNFORGIVABLE SIN?

Two questions often arise regarding professed Christians who commit suicide: First, could they be saved when they did not have the opportunity to confess their sin and seek forgiveness? Second, did they commit blasphemy, the unforgivable sin?

Regarding the opportunity to confess, passages like Romans 6:10 and Hebrews 10:10 make it clear that Christ died "once for all." This means that once a person has faith in Christ, all of that Christian's sin has already been atoned for—past, present, and future sin. When a Christian receives the grace of God, it is full grace. So just like Christians who die while committing any other sin (like theft or adultery), Christians who commit self-murder have indeed sinned but their Savior remains greater than their sin. Faith in him, not ongoing confession, is what saves.

On the matter of the unforgiveable sin, suicide is not that sin. The sin of blasphemy against the Holy Spirit is the sin of unbelief. It is the rejection of the Spirit's prompting to believe that Christ is Lord and that God raised him from the grave. All who by faith confess Christ as Lord and profess him as Savior will be saved, for this is the work of the Holy Spirit in a sinner's life. While friends and family will struggle with their loved one's suicide for obvious reasons, there is no biblical reason to believe those who die by suicide have automatically forfeited their salvation.

Those who profess Jesus Christ as Lord but commit suicide have, at least in that final moment, lost sight of the truth of the gospel. The gospel declares that a Christian is united to Christ in this very life. In the midst of the pain and anguish of life, it is imperative for Christians to be reminded of this glorious truth: the love God the Father gives to God the Son is the very same love that is delivered to the Christian through the indwelling Holy Spirit. This is not a cheap answer or an easy fix. It is possible that the person who commits suicide seemed like a genuine Christian but was never truly converted—but this should not be the default assumption. Life is hard, and mental illness is a tragic reality in this fallen world. This is why youth workers take students' mental health seriously: because anyone can fall into a spiritually dark place where their eyes have lost sight of God's face. These spiritually dark seasons are primed for hard conversations that might prove to be the moment when students realize the difference between faith in Jesus and simply believing the right things about him. But the truth of the gospel remains: Christians can live with hope because Jesus rose from the grave, ascended into glory, and will indeed return to complete the restoration of all things. This is the message of hope youth workers preach to students in their darkest moments.

So, the answer to the question is yes, those who commit suicide could have still been real Christians. But they do not commit suicide in order to claim gospel promises, but because they have lost sight of them.

PASTORAL CARE FOR STUDENTS WHO ASK ABOUT SUICIDE

There are no easy rules for how to comfort and minister to parents or students who may be suicidal or are grieving after a suicide. The following is presented to help you develop a plan moving forward:

Pray for wisdom. God is generous to those who ask (James 1:5). You may not feel equipped for this ministry, and that's okay—no one is. But God has provided you for these students or parents, and he will use you. Be confident in God and seek his wisdom.

Teach the gospel as more than a ticket to heaven. The gospel is the Christian's foundation for peace when they suffer ("Christ has overcome!"), joy when they are anxious ("You are dearly loved by your heavenly Father"), comfort when they are in danger ("Greater is he who is in you than he who is in the world"), and assurance of love when they feel unlovable ("Christ died for us while we were still sinners"). Proclaim the gospel without shame and with great confidence. Apply the gospel to every sphere of students' lives, not only their eternal destiny.

Listen carefully to what students are saying (and to what they're not). Most of the time, questions about suicide are quite unexpected. Pay attention to students' body language and other non-verbal cues. Listen carefully to how they word their questions (do they ask in first person or third person).

Ask gentle but direct questions about their intentions. It is usually best to clearly and directly ask students, "Are you thinking about hurting yourself?" Your tone and body language matter, but do not let a student ask about suicide without loving them enough to ask this direct and obvious question. Usually, they will expect you to ask it, and may be very confused (or even hurt!) if you don't ask. This question will also open up a conversation about why they brought up the topic—general curiosity, a friend who is struggling, or something else. If students confess they might hurt themselves, remember that youth workers are considered mandated reporters in most states and are obligated to report such concerns. See chapter 40.

Pray with them and follow up. The student has placed great trust in you by asking such a vulnerable question. As uncomfortable as it may be, contacting the student within the following days is good pastoral ministry. Don't let suicide be the only thing you talk about going forward, but a check-in or two in the next few days, and then again over the following weeks (assuming there are no red flags), will assure the student they are not walking alone.

Forge a partnership with their parents. If you asked a dozen youth pastors, I would expect them to be fairly divided on how much you should report to the students' parents. But if you desire to forge a true partnership with parents to co-evangelize and co-disciple their teenagers, how could you keep them uninformed about such a significant concern? It may be possible to tell parents about the conversation in broad strokes rather than telling them every specific thing—but they need to be aware this conversation took place.

16
Why Pray If God Will Do What He Wants?

P rayer is an integral part of the Christian life. God's people are instructed to intercede for others (2 Corinthians 1:11) and to make their requests known to God (Psalm 17:6). Christians pray with confidence, knowing that God is their heavenly Father who delights in giving good gifts to his children (Matthew 7:11) and that "if we ask anything according to his will he hears us" (1 John 5:14). Yet Christians may wonder why they should bother praying if God is sovereign—that is, in complete control over all things. This question is not beyond teenagers, and is an excellent discussion topic that helps them wrestle with the Bible and apply it to their daily faith.

WE PRAY *BECAUSE* GOD IS SOVEREIGN

We should first recognize that prayer is not undermined by God's sovereignty, but dependent on it. After all, if God is *not* sovereign, why pray? We pray and plead with God to grant our requests, like children plead with their father, because he is fully able to grant our requests.

For example, consider how we pray for the salvation of others. Ephesians 2:8 tells us salvation is outside of our control: "This is not your own doing; it is the gift of God." Yet at the same time, 1 Timothy 2:4 encourages us to pray for all people because God "desires all people to be saved." In his sovereignty, God invites us to pray and ask. We pray for our friends and family and enemies precisely *because* God is sovereign. Rather than giving into despair and futility, our prayers are fueled by confidence that God can truly change the most hardened hearts and stubborn wills.

If, as some say, God is a "gentleman," then he would simply be a bystander who looks on as humans write their own destinies, occasionally shouting advice from the bleachers. Instead, the Bible paints a different portrait: a God who is intimately and personally involved in calling, empowering, and using people to accomplish his good and perfect will. This gives us great courage to pray, believing that our God hears us and is able to act.

We Pray Because We Are God-Dependent Worshipers

We pray as an acknowledgment that we are not independent creatures. We are completely dependent on God, who provides. Yet in this dependent relationship with God we are children, not slaves. And so we come to him with requests, prayers, and offerings of thanksgiving and praise—as a natural overflow of our relationship. Rather coming before God to command him (like the clay shouting at the potter in Isaiah 45:9), we pray because we trust God as our loving, heavenly Father. This is why prayer becomes a struggle in those seasons when we lose sight of our need for God and instead begin to rely on our own ability to provide. Prayer is at the core of the Christian's relationship with God because, through it, faith is built, nurtured, and reinforced.

God does not always grant our requests. Those instances can easily tempt us to think about prayer as a battle between our desires and God's. It is imperative to help students realize the purpose of prayer is not just to get what we want. The question, "Why bother praying?" is a reminder of how selfishly we approach God. It is good to bring our requests before God, but if our prayers are only full of requests, we have turned God into the genie from *Aladdin*, hoping we have another wish left in the bank.

We must learn to come before God both with fear and trembling (because he is holy) and with confidence (because we are children of God). Studying the way God's people pray throughout Scripture is a much-needed reminder that prayer is about expressing faith and worship and gratitude to our holy God who has chosen to adopt us as sons and daughters. In Scripture, we see prayers of praise (Psalm 150), confession (Psalm 51), requests for help (Philippians 4:6), and intercession for others (James 5:15). Ultimately, we pray because God is holy and he is worthy of every breath we take. This is true even when our requests are answered with a no.

WE PRAY BECAUSE GOD COMMANDS IT

The simplest answer to the question of why we should we pray is this: God tells us to. The Bible consistently describes God's people as those who worship him and pray to him. God responds to the prayers of his people (see Daniel 10:12). Godly people are praying people because they know how much they rely on the Lord to provide and sustain them by his mercy.

If God has so loved us that he gave his Son, Jesus Christ, in order that we might become children of God, then surely we can trust his goodness and wisdom in those times when he chooses to not grant the response to prayer that we prefer. He is holy, and yet we are invited to come as children before our heavenly Father. Pray with confidence and trust his response.

17

Why Does God Allow Suffering?[7]

Another school shooting. A classmate dies in a senseless car accident. A friend is diagnosed with cancer. A tornado causes significant damage in town. Why? Why does God allow these things to happen?

Some Christians respond, "He doesn't. We allow suffering to happen by not being the church. If the church acted like the church, suffering would cease." At first glance, this resonates and seems helpful. It comforts, because it allows students to continue worshiping God without blaming him for evil. It inspires, because it motivates them to alleviate the suffering of those around them.

But it's also empty, because it doesn't address persecution or cancer or earthquakes or random accidents that cannot be prevented by the church "being the church." It also suggests that suffering is always opposed to God's will, and yet Scripture consistently presents suffering as the context for our sanctification and God's glory (Psalm 27; 1 Peter 1:6–7; James 1:2). And in an attempt to let God off the hook, it sets him in the bleachers as an onlooker rather than as the sovereign one who daily sustains his creation. This is beyond the debate about human freedom and God's sovereignty; it simply doesn't reflect the way the Bible speaks about suffering. God hardens Pharaoh's heart even while

Pharaoh hardens it too (Exodus 4:21; 8:32). God sends not only the rain but also the drought (Haggai 1:11). "Whatever the LORD pleases, he does" (Psalm 135:6).

Helping students unravel God's mysterious purposes for suffering can seem like an impossible task. Impossible, and yet the Lord graciously sends us to sit with students who have received a cancer diagnosis, to comfort those who mourn, and to point broken hearts to the cross and empty tomb.

EMBRACE THE TENSION

On the one hand, it is entirely right and biblical to tell students, "This isn't the way it's supposed to be." They already know the suffering they endure simply isn't right. We were made to experience the perfect peace of Eden, yet our thumbs are pricked by thorns and we are betrayed by our own bodies. The world has been turned inside out by sin.

On the other hand, there is great comfort in knowing "that for those who love God all things work together for good" (Romans 8:28). God's sovereignty and his goodness have not flickered, but continue to shine in their perfect brilliance. He sees our anguish and suffering. With great compassion and sensitivity, we point students' hearts to behold the Lord in the midst of their pain.

Sometimes suffering is clearly the result of sin (like a school shooting), and sometimes it "just happens" (like cancer). Other times it's a confusing mixture (car accidents, or a surgery gone wrong). It's important to grow in pastoral wisdom to discern the thoughts and feelings your students are likely wrestling with and give them permission to voice them. Let your presence speak more than your mouth does. Embrace this tension in your prayers while you mourn with those who mourn. And when you do speak, avoid theological lectures.

LOOK TO THE CROSS

The greatest comfort we offer students is to point them to the cross and empty tomb. When we look at the cross, we see God's sovereign grace shining through the greatest act of evil and suffering in human history. The second person of the Trinity was betrayed and abandoned by his friends, framed by the priests who were entrusted with the honor of leading God's people in worship, and then crucified among the vilest offenders of the day while the crowd mocked him. God understands suffering—not merely in theory, but in all its gritty agony.

At the foot of the cross, we see God's holiness (Jesus was the sinless, perfect Son of God), his love (he gave himself as our substitute), his power (he would conquer death by enduring it), and his wrath (he did not overlook the judgment sin deserves, but poured it out upon Jesus). It was God-ordained, and yet Judas and other conspirators remained guilty and responsible for their acts.

God's grace in suffering rings especially clear in Romans 8. First, we remind students that God is with us and he understands our suffering, since the Son himself has come "in the likeness of sinful flesh and for sin" (v. 3). Second, the way we endure suffering shows the world we are living for another kingdom that will surely come when Christ returns: "The sufferings of this present time are not worth comparing with the glory that is to be revealed to us" (v. 18). Third, we cling to hope that God is working out his plan of salvation despite our suffering, so that "all things work together for good" (v. 28). Finally, we live with cross-shaped endurance because God issued his judgment against sin and death through the cross and the empty tomb, and we share in that victory through faith. In all our sufferings, "we are more than conquerors through him who loved us" (v. 37).

When students suffer, remember that they need a big God. Shepherd them with gentle and tender care, but apologizing for God's sovereignty will only minimize their confidence that God can work his grace into their hearts even through their pain and tragedy. We serve a holy God whose ways are not our ways, and that is a good thing—because only God would devise a plan like the gospel to rescue sinners from a sinful and broken world.

SECTION 2
Practical Help for Youth Workers

18
Starting a Youth Ministry

"**W**here do we start?" is a question usually asked by either a small church with no budget for a paid youth worker or a church plant seeking to minister to the teenagers and parents in their growing church family. The good news is this: these churches have an incredible opportunity for deep and meaningful intergenerational ministry—a church-wide commitment to regularly (though not always exclusively) bringing the generations together for worship, discipleship, fellowship, and service. In some unique ways, this gives teenagers a greater opportunity to experience the riches of a church family than teenagers in a larger church will ever know.

This chapter is offered to point churches that are just getting started in the right direction quickly. Many of its core elements are distilled from my previous book, *A Biblical Theology of Youth Ministry: Teenagers in the Life of the Church* (Randall House Academic, 2019). Please consider that book an additional resource to help launch or recalibrate your church's ministry to students.

THE MOST HELPFUL QUESTION YOU CAN ASK

The best question a team of pastors, elders, and youth workers can ask is this: "What do we expect from a growing teenage

Christian in our church?" Sadly, the most common response is usually, "That's a great question. I've never thought about that before."

There is no better time to gain clarity on the role of teenage Christians in the local church than when you are launching a youth ministry. If you expect teenage Christians only to attend youth group, then building an attractive program will become your primary task. But if you want teenagers to joyfully worship the Lord, be discipled, serve the body, and minister to the community, then your new youth ministry will emphasize discipleship and intergenerational ministry. Clarity from day one is a significant advantage over ministries that are trying to make this shift after years of taking a different approach.

Asking what you expect from a growing teenager will likely slow down the timeline for launching your new ministry because it will cause you to be thoughtful and strategic. But this approach will pay significant long-term dividends.

PRINCIPLES FOR LAUNCHING A YOUTH MINISTRY

1. **Treat youth ministry as real ministry.** Youth ministry is more than a training ground for future leaders of other ministry areas. Recruit men and women who are godly and mature, whose faith and wisdom you want passed on to the next generation. Yes, youth ministry is a good place for young leaders to grow and develop, but this will only happen when it is real ministry that involves deep discipleship, growth in Christian community, evangelistic zeal, expository teaching, pastoral counseling, strategic leadership, and other essentials of real ministry. Resist the temptation to simply entertain students with the hollow conviction that Christians can have fun too.

2. **Always keep the gospel central.** Launching a youth ministry begins with prayerful deliberation about how to reach students with the gospel, not by gathering a list of fun games and events that will attract students. The gospel

shapes every facet of youth ministry, not only the way a church evangelizes. The goal is not to simply provide a safe space for students, but to see them transformed through the gracious promise of God. Fun and games are not the enemy, but the gospel belongs at the heart of every facet of ministry to students. This will affect the way you interact with students, empower them for ministry, comfort them in their heartbreaks—and even play games together. There is simply no greater gift to students than to always keep the gospel front-and-center.

3. **Make disciples.** Making disciples is the greatest thing your ministry can do. If you don't have any retreats or fancy swag or a trending social media account, that's okay! Start with the students God has given you and disciple them. Be faithful in mentoring the students you have rather than dreaming about those you don't. Resist the temptation to focus so much on developing a program that you rarely spend time helping students learn how to read the Bible and pray. Listen to them and allow them to wrestle with difficult questions. Equip them to grow in the Lord and minister to their friends.

4. **Build a team.** Don't do the ministry alone. This first leadership team you establish will set the tone for the future of the ministry, so be discerning about who to empower and be willing to graciously say no to others. Serving with a team always bears better long-term fruit than doing ministry alone. Starting with a team is more work and might frustrate leaders, because others may modify their vision. But they'll also have a team to carry the load.

5. **Partner with parents.** You might be tempted to try to give students a space away from their families. But unless there are parents who insist on taking control, partnering with parents is more likely a significant advantage. View this as an opportunity to equip parents to think biblically and theologically about evangelism and discipleship of adolescents. It is time for youth ministry to embrace parents

as legitimate youth workers who lead in these areas rather than only tapping them as drivers and food providers. Generally speaking, it will be best to empower parents to serve in the ministry while avoiding scenarios where they lead their own teen's small group.

6. **Be intergenerational.** Consider this case study:

> Amanda's family has been attending First Baptist Church since she was born. She happily participated in children's church, but began serving in the nursery when she was old enough since the sermons were difficult for her to understand. Other students felt the same, and their parents were distracted by their bored teenagers, so the church formed a Bible study to minister to the teenagers. Amanda enjoyed this alternative and fruit seemed evident in her life. Upon high school graduation, she attended a public university and connected with a campus ministry, but stopped attending church. Now that she is a college graduate, Amanda struggles to find a church where she feels a sense of belonging. She is still a professing Christian and occasionally reads her Bible, but does not often attend church.

   In many ways, modern children's and youth ministry set up children like Amanda to unplug from the church—because they were never a meaningful part of the church in the first place. The church was for their parents, and there were side offerings for kids like Amanda. If children and teenagers are not worshiping with the whole church, and if they never attend church functions where they are not the primary audience, they might experience a sense of belonging in the youth ministry—but not in the church.

7. **Think big, start small.** Think big about where you would like the ministry to grow, but start where you are. Look around, and discern the first small step in the right direction that's an easy win. Notice that this specifies a step *in the right*

direction. Often, the easiest first step is in line with the status quo. Don't do that. One little victory—a simple change to an existing program, or a single event that can give a foretaste of the type of change you hope to build—will clarify the direction you are heading while increasing trust and momentum to take your next step. As these victories stack up, you'll be well on your way. Along the way, keeping the big picture clear for everyone on the team will help you resist temptations to chase other good opportunities that pull you off course.

19
Attributes of a Great Youth Worker

A church might be able to run a youth program with paid staff members, but it cannot effectively disciple students without a strong team of volunteers. Since you're reading this book, you're probably interested in growing as an excellent youth worker! You want to know how to make a significant contribution to the ministry while being an outstanding team player, and also how to recruit new youth workers to join the team.

SHOULD PARENTS VOLUNTEER IN YOUTH MINISTRY?

Consider this scenario: A youth ministry is trying to serve as co-evangelist and co-discipler alongside parents, but there are no parents involved in the ministry or speaking into its leadership. Something should sound wrong about that situation, and yet it's remarkably common. There are two main solutions: prayerfully select a few parents who would serve well in the youth ministry, or intentionally create a way for regular planning, affirmation, and counsel between parents and youth workers.

Parents are often excellent youth workers. Not only do they have insider information about students' unfiltered opinions, they are highly motivated to reach their sons' or daughters' peers. It is a good policy for the youth pastor to have a personal conversation with a student prior to talking with that student's parent about serving in the youth ministry. You want to be sure the student will not feel cramped and therefore dread coming to youth group. Also look out for students who are especially close with their parents and need a space where other mature adults can provide pastoral care and guidance. It will be important for them to learn how to follow non-parental leadership.

A key trait to look for is parents who are committed to shepherding teenagers who aren't theirs. Parents who will only look after their own children and their children's friends will show favoritism that will breed an unhealthy culture in the ministry. This type of helicopter parenting can also bring a critical spirit between youth workers and students as parents get viewed as chaperones rather than as mentors. But parents who want to support fellow parents by ministering to their teenagers are an incredible gift to the church.

WHAT MAKES A GREAT YOUTH LEADER?

1. **Genuinely converted.** While this seems obvious, it isn't. It is surprisingly common for youth volunteers to attend student evangelism events and get converted alongside the students they are supposed to be leading. While no one can judge another person's heart, baptism and membership (or a similar denominational equivalent) is a good expectation to ensure that youth workers have given a credible profession of faith. If a youth worker is genuinely converted, but cannot clearly articulate the gospel in their first interview with the youth pastor, it is important to provide adequate coaching before they join the team. Using a resource like *The Gospel-Centered Life* during part of the interview process can help you get a sense of their spiritual life while equipping them with a gospel-vocabulary to employ in their ministry to students.

2. **Track record of godliness.** Recent converts seem like wonderful, energy-giving men and women to spark revival in a youth ministry. But instead of plugging them

into ministry, give them time to develop healthy rhythms of growth and maturity as their faith takes root. Youth workers set an example for the students they lead, so it is absolutely crucial for them to be men and women who are growing in godliness and maturity. Along with a credible profession of faith, this is of utmost importance.

3. **Relates well to teenagers.** This is a general rule of thumb: good youth workers talk with teenagers. Youth workers don't always need to be the life of the party, and they don't need to be cool or trendy. But good youth workers do invest the time and effort necessary to build trust and rapport with students. Staff your ministry with youth workers who connect with both extroverts and introverts.

4. **Keeps commitments.** A team of superstar leaders who rarely keep their commitments is a bad team. Teenagers need consistency, and a team needs to be able to rely on each other. For this reason, it is better to refuse a good youth volunteer until they are able to make a clear commitment. Of course, some work schedules can be irregular, and no youth worker will always be at everything. But a youth worker who consistently informs the youth pastor, "I won't be there tonight, sorry" can derail the entire plan for that night's meeting. It's valuable to have a formal application process so you can see whether or not the interested youth volunteer will complete the application and turn it in without being chased down. If they don't complete a simple application and turn it in, why should the team expect them to follow through when they volunteer to prepare a game or Bible study?

5. **Is available.** If a potential volunteer is so busy they need to make careful calculations about whether or not they can serve in your ministry, it is probably good pastoral care to encourage them to wait. Christians should not be so busy with work and life and ministry that there is no margin for rest. In your interview with the volunteer, ask how many hours a week they work and about their family, church, and

other commitments. Busy and stressed-out youth workers will have limited capacity to truly invest in students (who are also busy and stressed). It is better to have a smaller team of volunteers who last for the long haul than to burn through everyone who expresses interest.

6. **Receives correction well.** Mistakes happen. Good leaders embrace hard conversations when lines have been crossed and mistakes have been made. Youth workers who take every corrective word personally either will become so discouraged they will drop out of ministry or will become divisive. This is not a license for you to be an authoritarian leader, but it is a recognition that leadership involves correction. While interviewing a potential youth worker, it helps to ask, "How do you tend to handle correction? If something happens and we need to have a hard conversation, what should I know to ensure that is a healthy and constructive conversation rather than one that leads to conflict and damages our relationship?" Honest conversations about this question early in the partnership can do wonders to set up a long-term, fruitful partnership.

HOW TO RECRUIT NEW YOUTH WORKERS

Here is the best way I have been able to recruit youth leaders over the past fifteen years: Carry a small notebook or create a note in your phone that is easy to update, and ask for volunteer recommendations from the pastoral staff, other youth leaders, parents, and students. Keep track of the names and note who is mentioned multiple times. After you have prayed through the list of names, approach the person and say, "I've been praying for wisdom about growing our team of youth leaders, so I asked for recommendations from the church staff, other youth leaders, parents, and even students. Your name was mentioned multiple times. Would you prayerfully consider serving in the youth ministry? Unless your answer is an immediate no, I'd love for you to spend some time praying about this and talking about it with others, and we could meet in the next week or two to discuss it more. What do you think?" This removes the insecurity that is often present when someone considers working with teenagers, and conveys confidence that you believe the person can make a contribution to the ministry.

Having a simple application and interview process will serve you well. In your first meeting with a potential volunteer, get to know each other and share testimonies. In the second, talk about the youth ministry—why it exists, its driving values, its programs, and why are they structured the way they are—and the volunteer's potential involvement. If necessary, a third meeting can address questions and clarify expectations.

Finally, avoid making your youth team a group of like-minded friends. Your team should not only be as diverse as the students in your ministry, but also as diverse as the students you hope will be in your ministry twelve months from now. Your diverse team will end up forming a unique bond. Encourage one another and serve shoulder to shoulder, because the youth leaders set the tone for how students treat each other.

20
Fostering a Healthy Ministry Culture

Culture is the way a group behaves without thinking about it. The best way to identify and describe a ministry's culture is through careful observation. A gospel-centered youth ministry strives to cultivate an atmosphere of grace where students *experience* the same freedom and rest they hear the leaders proclaim through the gospel. Too much joking in a group can easily lead to biting sarcasm that keeps serious conversations from happening. But an absence of laughter probably means everyone is on edge, and either they're trying to be impressive or they don't want to be there.

AN ATMOSPHERE OF GRACE

Think about a place where you breathe a sigh of relief upon entering. You know you are among friends who genuinely care for you. You are welcomed. Façades and masks come down. Failures are treated as opportunities to learn and grow, not as moments of shame. Successes are celebrated and affirmed, but they aren't what makes you valuable and loved. You are free to simply be yourself—without fear of judgment and without the pressure to impress.

It might help to develop a culture-statement ("We are kind, forgiving, and thoughtful"), and even to paint it on the wall to keep it front-and-center. Just remember that students know if they are only words on a wall, or if they are truly a reflection of the culture that is developed and protected by the leaders in the group.

Incidents that require correction and disciplinary action are among the most influential culture-setters for any ministry. An atmosphere of grace does not eliminate discipline, but it shapes how discipline is communicated and carried out—and how the person is restored.

Consider the following example of what a gospel-centered culture can look like: It is common for youth workers to feel a sense of resentment about school sports teams—for good reason! When there is a schedule conflict between a student's basketball game or a youth-group event, the basketball team will almost always win the student's time. But what if this is an opportunity to extend grace rather than making the student feel like a bad Christian? If a student misses a few games, they may be kicked off the team. But if they miss youth group, they know they'll be welcomed back. Isn't that what we want? Instead of breeding competition between youth group and other activities, empower students to be your church's ambassador to their team or club. Attending their games to cheer them on reinforces this vision and so you can continue discipling students who then minister to their teams. This approach conveys the importance of youth ministry while covering students with grace when they are absent from group.

Culture Killers

- **Favoritism.** Students are savvy. They usually know who the leaders' favorites are in the group, and they know who's on the outside. When leaders consistently grant special privileges to a select few, the culture will suffer. Youth workers will obviously connect with certain students better than others, but they must be very careful to treat every student equally in group meetings, and to resist the temptation to only spend time with students they prefer. Overt favoritism can wreak havoc on a youth group's culture, but beware that even perceived favoritism can erode trust within the group.

- **Cliques.** While favoritism can blow up the group's culture from the leadership, cliques can spread division like gangrene among students. It's wonderful when youth group becomes the context for friendships to blossom. The key way a friend group is different from a clique is that outsiders are truly welcomed in, not just reluctantly allowed to join for a few moments. Cliques usually make themselves known through inside jokes and by dressing similarly. When a clique begins to make others feel excluded and unwelcomed, it is wise to talk with the students involved early in the process to invite them to promote the group's atmosphere of grace.

- **Sarcasm.** One of the more common dysfunctions in a youth group culture shows up when there is no distinction between friendly joking and sarcastic barbs. Sarcasm seems prevalent among longtime youth workers. But when students don't know if your words of encouragement are genuine or if they should brace for the punchline, you need to seriously tone down the sarcasm. Most of the time, sarcasm is a self-defense mechanism used to keep others from getting too personal—and that's the opposite of the posture youth workers want to have toward students. It may help to remember that the word *sarcasm* comes from a Greek word that means "to tear flesh." Healthy youth group cultures build one another up rather than tear each other down.

- **Permissive leadership.** Youth workers want all students to feel welcomed and accepted by the group—even the disrespectful troublemakers. But extending grace upon grace to those students by overlooking their toxic behavior does not actually extend grace to them; it puts them in the driver's seat of the entire group culture by letting them set the tone for what's acceptable. The most consistently disrespectful student in your ministry is setting the bar for your group's culture. It is an act of grace to the entire group to correct students who are out of line, issue some form of discipline in coordination with their parents or guardians, and develop a plan for how they can be reintegrated into the group.

- **Relational guilt.** Relational guilt usually happens when youth leaders make students feel like they will be hurting their leaders' feelings or damaging their relationship by not participating in promoted youth-group activities. When students are away from youth group for a period of time and return to be asked by youth leaders, "Where have you been?" they will immediately feel defensive and guilty. Invite students to participate. Tell them why it is valuable for them to be invested. But if they don't attend, resist the temptation to tell them how great it was and how much you missed them. Instead, take an interest in what they did. Guilting students into participation is usually accidental, but youth workers should be careful to avoid this pitfall.

- **Spiritual manipulation.** Spiritual manipulation is most frequently seen in evangelistic settings. A speaker might build trust with students by making them laugh, build empathy by making them cry, and then highlight the pain and suffering Jesus endured on the cross. This is spiritual manipulation because it makes students feel like they're letting God down by making Jesus's sufferings meaningless if they don't make a decision to follow him. Even worse, these emotionally-driven decisions have little foundation in any genuine conviction of sin and true repentance. When this is common in a ministry, students will eventually realize they are being spiritually manipulated and will (rightly) stop coming. The gospel calls us to be faithful shepherds to students, not to manipulate them so they do what we want. Preach the gospel and make disciples. It's much slower and won't showcase the same flashy results, but it bears fruit that lasts.

Helpful Questions to Ask about Your Group's Culture

Culture is best discerned by your own observation first and discussion with fellow observers later. Spend some time reflecting on these questions individually, then discuss them as a team. At a later stage, you may benefit from having someone visit for a few weeks who can give an outsider's perspective.

- Who's the hero of the group? Who's the villain of the group?
- Whose voice do I hear often? Who is being silent?
- Why do people laugh? Are they laughing together, or at each other's expense?
- Are the leaders treated with both respect and familiarity, or only with one or the other?
- How do we carry out correction and discipline?

21

Fun and Games in Youth Ministry

Fun and games have become an increasingly polarizing topic for youth workers to discuss. Some ministries appear to make them the highest priority, so that if something isn't exciting they simply won't do it. Others are skeptical of games because, as these youth workers love to remind everyone, youth ministry needs more than pizza and dodgeball. The rest of us are caught in the middle, feeling misunderstood by those on both extremes. This can make a productive conversation about fun and games more difficult than it should be.

It's hard to weep with students who weep and rejoice with students who rejoice when you can't even laugh together. Fun and games in youth ministry should never be about the fun and games at all. Instead, fun and games are instruments to craft and reinforce a group culture where students are welcomed. Welcomed to simply be. Welcomed to rest from trying to be someone they're not. Welcomed to make friends with peers who attend rival schools they've been trained to jeer and root against. Welcomed to interact with adults who genuinely care for them, despite all the teenage angst and drama. Welcomed to see the ways that Christians compete differently because they have been marked by grace rather than the belief that you are what you accomplish.

Fun and games can tear down the walls that keep students separated from each other, or they can build those walls higher.

While youth workers affirm that fun and games are not the enemy, they must also be aware that you can fail at fun and games by having too much of them.

WARNING SIGNS THAT FUN HAS OVERTAKEN YOUR MINISTRY

- **You are constantly searching for new and better games.** Obviously, it's good to play new games and to keep yourself from boring routines. But if you feel the pressure to impress your students with how much fun your group is and how creative your games are, then you're going about this all wrong. When you win students to your group *with* fun and games, then you've won them *to* fun and games. That's a deadly spiral you need to escape as soon as possible (probably by going cold turkey with no games for a month to clean the system before reintroducing games with a corrected posture). Try new things, but not at the expense of shortchanging your Bible study, lesson prep, or time with students.

- **Everything needs to be fun.** There is a time for fun, and a time to be serious. Mission team meetings don't need to place a high emphasis on fun. Remember that spending time with people you like can make anything fun, even if it's kind of boring, but playing a really fun game can still be a disaster if you're playing it with people you don't like. If you need to play games for students to have fun, the problem isn't a lack of games but the group culture. This is why a constant demand for "more fun" is symptomatic of broader dysfunction in the youth ministry—it's not about the games being "not fun;" it's an indicator about their relationship with other students in the group. For example, discipleship groups and service projects aren't always entertaining, but they are meaningful expressions of community within a healthy ministry.

- **Students are always asking, "What's the game tonight?"** There will always be some students who ask this question. But if this is the go-to question your more spiritually mature kids are asking, you might have a problem. If you need to promote the game via social media to get students to show up, you are drawing kids with the wrong thing. If students only come because they know their favorite game is on the docket, it is fair for you to ask whether the game or the gospel is front-and-center.
- **Your resources are disproportionately directed toward fun and games.** How do you spend your budget? What percentage of time gets allocated to meaningful discussion of Scripture compared to games? If someone looked at your meeting space, what would they say is the priority there? Where your treasure (your time, budget, scheduled programs, etc.) is, there your heart will be also.

Best Practices for Leading a Fun Ministry that Makes Disciples

1. **Don't forget that introverted nerds like to have fun too.** Their definition of fun doesn't always fit the youth-group mold. If the only games your group ever plays are athletic games, don't be surprised when all the non-athletes feel left out. Incorporate some thinking and strategy games, and couch games that are more accessible to quieter students.
2. **Realize that some games are simply too much fun.** Certain games will make doing anything spiritual afterward extremely difficult. Maybe the game takes a long time, so you have to cut your lesson short. Or maybe students are frustrated because their team was winning when the rules suddenly changed in order to bring about a quick ending to the game, and their team lost. Or maybe they're simply

sweaty and tired from all that running around. The reality is, some games are so fun they're best kept for game nights when all you're going to do is have fun.

3. **Understand that pranks are always a bad idea, and never shame a student.** In my early days of ministry, I played a game-night prank on a student. It was hilarious, but it was very shaming and embarrassing for that student. I chose him because we had a good relationship and he laughed it off. But I've regretted that prank ever since, and some visitors who never returned told the friends who brought them, "Why would I want to join a group that does that to each other?" Don't trade your trustworthiness for some laughs. It's not worth it.

4. **Pay attention to how you form teams.** Remember, fun and games are a great way for students to create shared experiences with peers they rarely interact with. But allowing groups of friends to compete against other groups of friends will only breed greater division. It's not terrible to occasionally allow friends to be on the same team, but mix it up. For example, if you have students form four parallel lines, one week you could make each line be a team, the next week you could make each row of four be a team, and other weeks students could be partnered with the person standing beside or behind them.

5. **Keep the rules simple.** When teenagers are excited to play a game, their ears turn off. The more complicated the rules are, the more you'll need to rehearse in order to present them as briefly and clearly as possible. Have a good communicator clearly give the rules, but not until all chatter has ceased and everyone is listening. Repeating the rules multiple times is a great way to sabotage a good game before it's even begun. If the rules are too elaborate, change them or save the game for a special game night.

6. **Recruit your more competitive leaders and students to help choose and lead the games.** This lets you coach them about *why* you play games in youth group, and you can help them

embrace the value of different types of games. Not only is this a good way to cultivate leadership and shared ministry in others, it will often make them better participants in other weeks because they have experienced how difficult it can be to lead a game.

7. **Explain your philosophy of games to the parents.** Every parent wants their kid to have fun at youth group. If a teenager comes home complaining that it was boring for a few weeks in a row, you might find a group of disgruntled parents begin to grumble. But if you can share your vision for fun and games as instruments for building a welcoming culture, that's something the parents can latch onto and appreciate. And when their kids complain about the game, Mom or Dad can support you and reinforce a healthy view of fun and games.

22
Understanding Gen Z's Religious Worldview

Among Gen Z, the generation born in the mid-nineties and later, tolerance is the new Golden Rule, safety is the new American dream, and those who fail to uphold either of these values should be "canceled." Being canceled means that person or group has forfeited their right to be tolerated because they have threatened others' emotional or physical safety. This extends to all areas of life, including religion and spirituality. For example, religion should promote everyone's personal pursuit of happiness, regardless of what those aspirations might be. Those who don't should be rejected because they impose their values on others. To Gen Z, justice means empowering people's self-expression. Anything that seeks to correct someone's aspirations or call them to repentance is therefore promoting injustice and should not be tolerated. They will be canceled.

This means youth workers can no longer assume any familiarity with the Bible or agreement with biblical teachings the way previous generations could assume the existence of God, the reality of sin and eventual judgment, and a basic code of right and wrong. Today, one in four teens believes morality changes over time, and nearly as many say it depends on each individual's beliefs. One in three claims no religious affiliation. Every study on Gen Z religious views agrees that atheism is on the rise while adherence to organized religion is down. The foundation of truth has been replaced with skateboards: each person stands on their own platform for truth, but even that rolls and shifts depending on their cultural surroundings.

The book of Judges repeats the refrain, "In those days there was no king in Israel. Everyone did what was right in his own eyes" (Judges 17:6; 21:25). This gives youth workers great hope because it is a reminder that these are not unprecedented times. God will establish a faithful remnant, and he will build his church through the grace and power of the gospel.

MINDFULNESS AND GOD-WITHIN

The earlier generation, millennials, are known for the phrase, "I'm spiritual, but not religious." Gen Z, however, is increasingly neither—at least, not spiritual in the traditional sense. Spirituality is alive and well in the form of mindfulness. Many public schools have begun promoting this practice in an effort to alleviate students' anxiety and help them mentally prepare for learning. Mindfulness exercises include some helpful practices like paying attention to one's breathing and silent meditation, but they also incorporate Eastern and New Age meditation practices that encourage students to tap into their inner energies and find their power within.

In this way, Gen Z spirituality exchanges transcendence for immanence. Gen Z isn't trying to connect with a higher power, but with god-within. The spirituality of mindfulness seeks only self. It reflects the postmodern shift where truth and meaning are defined by the individual.

CHRISTIAN UNIVERSALISM: A MOUNTING THREAT TO THE GOSPEL

Grace is at the heart of the gospel, and we certainly want to affirm that Christians are justified and find acceptance before God because of the work of Christ and not by their own merit. And yet, there is a mounting threat whereby students combine the tolerant worldview of their generation with this Christian gospel in order to affirm a belief called Christian universalism.

Christian universalism seems to affirm the gospel but is a deadly heresy. It teaches that all people everywhere will be saved because of Jesus's death and resurrection, even if they have never placed their faith in him. It says atheists, Muslims, Hindus, and everyone else share in the gospel's promise of salvation. This viewpoint is on the rise among Christian teenagers who have grown up believing the gospel while living in a hyper-tolerant culture. Students who embrace this false gospel may continue to consider themselves Christians, attend church with their parents, and participate in youth group while raising very few suspicions.

Youth workers can accidentally slip into promoting Christian universalism if they preach the gospel of grace but only rarely mention God's wrath and judgment. No one wants to come off as a doom-and-gloom Christian, and surely the gospel does offer students hope and joy in the midst of this anxious and depressed generation, so it is entirely good and biblical to emphasize the grace of God. But it is absolutely crucial that youth workers also make sure students understand that wrath and judgment are God's holy response to sin. If youth workers never call students to repentance, the odds are increasingly high that the students will take on the views of Christian universalism.

Jesus makes Christianity unique. He was not merely a great teacher or philosopher with great insight into the human condition. Jesus is God-in-flesh, and yet he died on the cross as the substitute for sinners. Students' hope is not found by practicing mindfulness, becoming the best possible version of themselves, or through perfect youth group attendance. Ultimately, Jesus is the only hope Christianity has to offer that cannot be found elsewhere.

GOSPEL ON-RAMPS FOR GEN Z

Gen Z is passionate about important values that can serve as reliable on-ramps to the gospel. One of the clearest points of entry for the gospel highlights our need for grace. This is a generation that is told "you are what you do," and students see the preferential treatment given to those who are smart, athletic, beautiful, or privileged. But the gospel declares grace to all who confess their need for Christ (not only to those who are considered worthy).

This is a generation whose music cries out for hope. Preaching the broader gospel of salvation history anchors students in a worldview that looks this world's brokenness in the eye with the blood-bought hope of Jesus Christ.

In a time when everything seems created to be outdated within a few years, the promise of true and lasting joy resonates with teenagers' hearts. When students befriend older Christians who can share the joy they've experienced despite intense suffering, they can be rooted in a joy that goes deeper than their troubles.

As the most racially diverse generation in American history, teenagers are uniquely poised to appreciate the ethnic and cultural diversity of the body of Christ. The gospel teaches us that we are all in need of a Savior and when we come to him in faith, we all become God's family. We are now sisters and brothers and that should override all that divides us. Help students to recognize the gospel as God's mission to rescue and unite all people groups as one diverse family, united in worship of their Holy God.

One of the greatest blessings of the younger generation is the way they force older generations to recognize injustices that have been overlooked or tolerated for far too long. As chapter 5 addresses, anyone who cares about justice and injustice needs to recognize the goodness of God's judgment. Despite their claims for tolerance, there are certain behaviors that Gen Z simply will not tolerate. Instead of throwing this inconsistency in their face, embrace it as a conversation about evil being a real thing, and if God is a good God then he must judge evil. From there, it is a clear on-ramp to presenting the gospel where sinners receive grace through faith in Jesus Christ.

God's Word does not change, but culture does. Youth workers don't need to be trendy in order to reach teenagers with the gospel, but they do need to take a posture toward Gen Z that says, "Your culture and worldview is worthy of my respect." Assuming a gracious posture toward Gen Z's religious worldview along with a good understanding of these gospel on-ramps will open up fruitful conversations about faith and life and eternity.

23
Mentoring and Discipling Students

The goal of youth ministry is not to build teenage disciples, but adult disciples whose faith took root in their teen years. Healthy ministries operate with this long-term vision for life-long faith instead of chasing short-term results. Youth workers sacrifice so much of themselves to invest in students, and it is heartbreaking to watch students walk away from the faith in the years following graduation. So be clear about what discipleship is and how to do it.

Discipleship is the process by which a student learns from and becomes like his or her teacher. It cannot be confined to a classroom, but has more in common with a craftsman's workshop where a master is training an apprentice. Discipleship is embodied teaching, not simply a transfer of information.

Effective discipleship requires both a disciple maker and a committed disciple. Youth workers have different passions and skill sets. Not every youth worker will be a gifted disciple maker, but each volunteer should know how their contribution to the ministry fuels the discipleship process. Make sure those who are actively discipling students are also being discipled and ministered to, lest they become spiritually exhausted or arrogant.

However, the most common misfire in youth ministries has to do with the second requirement: committed disciples. Out of a desire for all students to be discipled, reluctant and uncommitted students are sometimes paired with a mentor even though they remain disinterested. You simply cannot disciple a student who isn't interested. But when a few students catch a vision for discipleship, it is good to invest in them beyond what you are doing for others. This isn't favoritism, but a biblical commitment to discipleship.

Even the most gifted disciple makers can only enter into an intentional discipling relationship with a few students at a time. Understand that mature believers in the local church have always played a central role in the discipleship of the next generation as they transitioned from childhood into adulthood.[8] So, cast a vision for a wide array of mature Christians in the church to minister to students as they grow in the faith. Without a group of disciple makers to mentor students, it is disingenuous to fault the next generation for walking away from the faith. There was no one to disciple them!

THE CORE ELEMENTS OF A DISCIPLESHIP PLAN

Throughout Christian history, there have been three core elements to discipleship: Christian doctrine, Christian living, and Christian spirituality. Respectively, these have been taught through three frameworks: the creeds, the Ten Commandments, and the Lord's Prayer.

The early creeds of the church are statements of essential Christian belief, written down for believers to recite together to celebrate their shared faith in God. These include the Apostles' Creed, Creed of Nicaea, Nicene-Constantinopolitan Creed, Chalcedonian Creed, and Athanasian Creed. These five creeds are accepted by nearly every branch of Christianity as listing essential Christian beliefs, and rejection of their statements reflects heretical and unchristian doctrine. If these creeds contain the time-tested, essential doctrines of Christianity, why would youth workers *not* use them to teach doctrine to students? While discipleship is about more than theological knowledge, students must be taught certain theological truths in order to develop a mature and biblical faith. Any ministry would only benefit from incorporating the content of the creeds into their teaching ministry and discipleship process. If teenagers can handle AP Algebra, they can learn about the Trinity.

The Ten Commandments have been taught throughout Christian history to instruct believers about Christian ethics and morality. Although Christians "are not under law, but under grace" (Romans 6:14), Jesus affirmed the teachings of the law and expanded on the Ten Commandments in his Sermon on the Mount—giving us a portrait of God's people. Christian maturity means the believer's life reflects the character and glory of God. This applies to a student's life at home, at school, in the locker room, with friends, among enemies, on social media, and in private. Students saved by grace are called to live differently because the gospel has given them a new heart that desires to obey God. The Ten Commandments and Sermon on the Mount provide a solid foundation for discipling students into faithful, cross-shaped living.

The third component of historic Christian discipleship is the Lord's Prayer, not because it is a magical incantation to recite but because Jesus gave it after his disciples asked him to teach them how to pray. The elements of the Lord's Prayer reflect daily life with God—praising, hoping, trusting, asking forgiveness, fighting temptation. Neglecting to teach about the normal Christian life can lead students to assume the Christian life is supposed to be one big spiritual high. Students who do not pray regularly or read the Bible will never feed their soul and become mature Christians. Believers who learn the right doctrines and behaviors without practicing the spiritual disciplines often turn into the worst types of leaders in the church because they have all the appearances of Christianity but no real spirituality. Youth workers might shy away from practicing the spiritual disciplines with students, thinking they should not practice their righteousness in front of others (Matthew 6:1), but this is a false concern.

Spirituality is an essential element of modeling for students how to grow in faith.

When student leadership is part of the discipleship process, it creates teachable moments when theology shapes the way students live as disciples in this world. Youth workers have an important pastoral role in students' lives to help them learn the creed, commandments, and spirituality in a way that sends them into the world as Jesus's disciples. Student leadership provides opportunities for them to trust God by doing ministry that leads others to Jesus. This is an important part of the discipleship process, otherwise discipleship is merely educational. Invite them to lead and serve in ways that are appropriate, given their age and spiritual development. Set them up for success but allow them to struggle in order that they might see God provide while learning from their failures. Encouraging students to trust God through the risk of stepping out in ministry is part of the discipleship process, whether it's a new Christian sharing their faith for the first time or a mature believer sharing their testimony in youth group.

WHAT DO I TEACH WHEN?

In 1 John 2:12–14, John provides spiritual guidance to new Christians ("children"), growing Christians ("young men"), and mature Christians ("fathers"). We can break down the passage to get a suggested guide for youth workers as they consider how to disciple students into maturity. Realize that very few Christians reach maturity during their teen years, so do not be discouraged if most students are either disinterested in discipleship or are in stage one or two.

New Christians: "I am writing to you, little children, because your sins are forgiven for his name's sake" (v. 12).
- Clarity on the gospel
- The overarching story of the Bible: creation, fall, redemption, glorification
- How to pray and understand the Bible

- Why membership in a local church is important
- Significant areas where the gospel calls for repentance in their lives
- The basics of evangelism

Growing Christians: "I write to you, young men, because you are strong, and the word of God abides in you, and you have overcome the evil one" (v. 14).
- Essential Christian doctrines (creeds)
- Connecting the overarching story of the Bible with worldview formation. How the gospel guides students' whole lives—home, school, recreation, friendships, social media, and private life.
- Ongoing counsel on walking in repentance and obedience to Christ
- Increasing knowledge on how to evangelize and answer objections to Christianity
- Cultivating regular spiritual disciplines in private

Mature Christian: "I write to you, fathers, because you know him who is from the beginning" (v. 14).
- Ability to articulate essential Christian doctrines
- Widening scope of complex Christian thought
- Basic ministry training and ongoing leadership development
- Empowerment to continue the disciple-making process by ministering to new believers

With these elements in mind, remember that discipleship doesn't happen in a vacuum. It happens when disciple makers teach their disciples through both instruction and demonstration.

How to Prioritize Discipleship over "Hanging Out"

1. **Seek both quality time and quantity of time.** Quality time can't be scheduled; it happens spontaneously while spending time together. Youth workers are always seeking

teachable moments to point students to Christ, and that often requires an investment of time: going to their games, concerts, or performances, and other similar efforts to meet students on their turf. Never underestimate the ministry of being present.

2.   **Teach through demonstration.** As youth workers hang out with students, they should be aware that everything they do teaches something: how they speak to waiters and cashiers, the way they talk about family members, even what makes them roll their eyes. I don't write that to create pressure to always be "on" or to feel the need to perform for students, but rather to give assurance that even when no "spiritual" conversations have taken place, a youth worker has still taught something.

3.   **Ask good questions.** Students expect to be asked about their prayer life and other spiritual topics, so ask them. But instead of asking predictable questions, ask thoughtful ones that invite students to open up.

4.   **Make an intentional plan with the student for discipleship.** Being casual about discipleship can sometimes lead to uncertainty and a lack of follow-through. When students demonstrate a willingness and teachable spirit to be discipled, talk with them about the subjects you'd like to study with them, and agree on a plan.

24

Preparing a Bible Message

I t is surprisingly common for youth workers who affirm the authority, inspiration, and inerrancy of Scripture to lead their ministries as if the Bible is not effective for teenagers. But the Word of God is never powerless. If God has spoken through the Bible (and we call it the Word of God for a reason!) and if we want our students to hear from the Lord, then we must lead with an unwavering commitment to teach the Bible. When we do, we find relief from the pressure to hit a home run every time we teach, because the Holy Spirit is always at work when his Word is taught.

This chapter will help you understand a biblical text so you are ready to teach it, and the next chapter will help you craft and deliver your message in a way that effectively connects with your students. I highly recommend buying a nice notebook to dedicate to message preparation, or creating a folder in your computer for your Bible study preparation.

PREPARATION: FOUR QUESTIONS TO ASK OF THE TEXT

The following four questions will equip you to prepare biblically-faithful messages that set an example for your students about how to read and study the Bible. Working your way through these four questions are crucial preparation to ensure your teaching is anchored in Scripture:

1.   What? (Original meaning). This first question anchors Bible reading in the context of the writer and the original readers. It requires the most effort and time, because it takes work to understand the ancient world. You'll need to consider the social context of the day and explore biblical themes that pertain to the passage. Investing in a good study Bible and bookmarking some helpful websites will serve you well as you work through this step. Some questions you may want to consider:

- How might the passage be summarized in one or two sentences?
- If it's a story, who are the main characters and what is their role in the action? If not, who wrote this passage and who was it written for?
- What was the author's goal in writing this?
- What comes before and after this portion of Scripture, and how does that affect its message?
- What keywords are repeated? Or, what keywords in this passage are significant throughout the Bible?
- How does the genre (poetry, history, prophecy, letter, etc.) influence the way you read this passage?

2.   So what? (Universal meaning). Now it's time to discern the passage's message. Refrain from immediately jumping to personal application. Instead, look for ways the original audience was being encouraged, rebuked, instructed, or warned.

- Why was this included in Scripture when so many other stories or truths were not?
- What does this passage reveal about who God is, who we are, what God has done, and what he calls us to do?
- How does this passage foreshadow, tell, or flow out from the gospel?
- What is the message of this passage that remains true for Christians today?

3. Now what? (Applied meaning for your students). It is now time to prayerfully consider how this text invites you to respond. Because the Bible is not merely an instruction manual for life, we must resist turning every verse into a new law that always tells students to try harder. As you teach God's Word, consider students' objections to its message, grapple with the text's invitation to students in your group, and lead them to Jesus.

- Where does this passage call me to repent of sin, to confess daily faith in God's holiness and grace, and to live by faith?
- What kind of application does this passage call for: head (correct my thinking about God or myself), heart (ways my emotions and desires have gone astray), or hands (a sin I need to stop doing, or something godly I have left undone)?
- How does this message relate to what we see in youth culture? In what ways does this promise true fulfillment of something our world promises but can't deliver? Where does this passage correct or redeem what we see in culture?
- What would it look like for a teenager to live in light of this passage?
- How is this passage calling me to warm my heart to the work of God through Jesus Christ?

4. Where's the gospel? The Bible tells one unified story: the work of God in creating a people for himself. This story can be traced from Genesis through Revelation in motifs like creation, the image of God, covenant, temple, exodus, kingdom, and others. The message of the gospel runs through each of these themes, as the narrative of Scripture tells of the unfolding salvation of God's people. Therefore, it is important to see how each verse has a place in God's work of salvation.

- How does this passage show our need for the gospel?
- How is the new life we have because of the gospel reflected in this passage?

- Where does this passage fit in the framework of creation, fall, redemption, and glorification?
- Which facet of the gospel does this passage emphasize: the purpose for which we were created, the nature and effects of sin, anticipation of salvation (or warnings to those who refuse it), the person and work of Jesus, what the Christian life looks like because of Jesus, consummation of salvation when Jesus returns to complete our salvation and bring judgment on sin?

IDENTIFYING THE BIG IDEA

The four questions above provide the biblical foundation for your teaching, but do not teach *everything* you unearthed in your preparation. You do not need to show your homework to prove that your message is biblical. Instead, identify the main point of the passage, discern the gospel connection, and consider how to convey that message to students in a way that is clear and helpful. Your message should be clearly anchored in the biblical text without being a regurgitation of your study. Ask yourself these questions:

- What is the central verse, teaching, or theme that holds this portion of Scripture together?
- What is the most important thing in this passage that you must teach in order to confidently say, "I was faithful to say what the text says."
- How can you clearly teach the central point of this text in one sentence?

Remember, God's Word is powerful and effective. This is true in the youth room every bit as much as it is in the pulpit.

25

Teaching Students and Keeping Their Attention

Teaching is hard work, especially when there is a room full of angsty teenagers who feel like they've already heard what you have to say. Speaking clearly while managing distractions and reading the atmosphere of the room, all while keeping eye contact and maintaining good non-verbal communication, can take a lot of effort. Good teachers never stop learning. This usually involves asking for loving critique. So whether you're a fearful rookie or a seasoned veteran, take an honest evaluation and ask the Lord to help you develop as a teacher. Your goal, leading students to be transformed by the good news of Jesus Christ, is an excellent motivation.

It is essential to work through the questions in the previous chapter *prior* to crafting your message, or what you teach will only have a biblical veneer rather than being deeply anchored in God's authoritative Word. Build off your notes from studying the text (remember the recommendation to answer the questions from the previous chapter in a notebook or computer document), giving extra attention to applying Scripture to their head, heart, and hands. Ensuring students can see how your message connects with their daily lives will help keep their attention. Pray for discernment.

Your goal will be to open students' eyes to behold the grace of God poured out for them through Jesus Christ and for them to respond with genuine faith. This means resisting the temptation to include everything you've unearthed in your preparation. Instead, highlight the big idea of the biblical text. If you are committed to expository teaching, you will cover a wide range of biblical truths rather than repeating certain hobbyhorses, so it's okay to focus on the main point of the text and leave other points for another week.

Now, let's explore how to deliver God's Word in a way that will connect with students and keep their attention.

USE ILLUSTRATIONS WELL

Illustrations come in many forms—stories, metaphors, quotations, movie references, jokes—and can be a wonderful on-ramp for your listeners to connect with your message. In many ways, illustrations are like commercials: they may portray the significance of the message and pique the listener's interest, or they might be so clever and entertaining that the listener forgets the point. Not everything that's memorable is good or useful.

Most illustrations fail because they're dead on arrival. They were poorly conceived, or are too long, or they rely on insider knowledge shared only by a select group of people, or they're simply delivered in a way that commands no interest. Others fail because they are so vivid or funny that they overtake their intended point and students become more captivated by the illustration than the message. Resist the pull toward illustrations to entertain or merely to keep attention. Use them to help students understand, see, hear, and feel the importance of what God's Word is saying to them.

The best illustrations do not teach, they uncover. An opening illustration can help students realize they already have opinions about the point of tonight's message. Another illustration can help students see the ways their lives already reflect the big idea you are emphasizing. Good illustrations connect something already present in the listener's life to the biblical message you are teaching.

EXAMPLE OF A TRIED-AND-TRUE TEACHING TEMPLATE

It is especially helpful for new teachers to have a simple framework around which they can build their message. The best-known speaking template for youth ministry is probably Hook-Book-Look-Took.[9] As you discover your own teaching voice, feel free to create alternative models for your messages, so long as you are seeking honest feedback from others about whether or not your messages are connecting with students.

Hook: Start off with a short illustration or story that introduces the theme of your talk.

Book: Read the Scripture passage you will be teaching.

Look: Explore the big idea of the text and help students see the truth and power of God's Word. This portion of the message is often the longest.

Took: Apply the big idea to their head, heart, and hands so students can take the message home. Resist the temptation to make this only one or two sentences at the end of your message. Instead, weave applications throughout your message so you can emphasize them with greater power at the end.

There is no universally right answer to the question of how long to speak. It depends on both your speaking ability and the group's attention span. Generally, the younger your students are, the closer to fifteen minutes you should stay; and the more experienced you are as a teacher, the closer you can stretch to thirty minutes. Within that timeframe, honestly evaluate your effectiveness as a teacher and the attention span of your students.

TECHNICAL SPEAKING SKILLS

One of my preaching professors taught that we should pay attention to the Four P's: *Pitch, Pause, Pace,* and *Punch*. When your *pitch* rises and falls, this keeps you from being monotone. Using a well-timed *pause*, usually after saying your big idea or something that will take an extra second or two before it sinks in, will serve your listeners well. Sometimes your main point is well-emphasized by speeding up your *pace*, other times by slowing down and letting your students lean into what you have to say. And *punch* means accentuating a keyword for emphasis. This doesn't happen by shouting or yelling, but by giving a certain word (or a certain syllable) slightly extra *umph* to make it stand out.

Also be aware of your filler words and annoying tics. I cannot wear a watch while I teach, or it becomes a fidget toy. I can be prone to saying the words *like, so*, and *right* when I stray from my notes. Because people have made me aware of these bad habits (and have listened to recordings of my messages), I can be thoughtful about avoiding them. When you find yourself about to fall into one of these habits, just take an extra second to pause, collect your thoughts, smile, and then move on. If you aren't aware of your tics or annoying habits, ask some people you trust to speak honestly and gently with you. I'm sure they've noticed a few if they've heard you teach more than half a dozen times.

Don't Assume the Gospel

Finally—and this cannot be emphasized enough—resist the temptation to assume the gospel. This can happen when you simply talk about "the gospel" without explaining what it is and anchoring your message in it. Assuming the gospel usually means you've suspected that everyone in the audience either is a Christian already or has heard the gospel so many times they don't want to hear it again. So you give in to the pressure to come up with something fresh and new that will capture students' attention.

You will never preach an original sermon—and if you do, it's probably some ancient heresy wrapped up in modern clothing. If you are bored with the gospel, maybe it would be better for you to take a break from teaching so someone else can step in and allow you space to revive your intimacy with Jesus. Always lead students to Jesus, and study biblical theology enough that you know how to do that in a way that isn't the same message every week. When we begin to assume the gospel, we stop proclaiming it.

26
Leading Effective Small Groups

Discipleship takes place best through relationships. That means your ministry will likely involve some kind of small-group ministry. Whether your entire youth group is a small group, or you meet informally with a few students outside of youth group, or you have a well-formed small-group infrastructure, there are basic skills every small-group leader needs.

Small groups matter because they create space for students to get real with each other and with God. At their best, small groups become a safe place to talk openly about sin, doubts, and struggles as students wrestle with their faith and grow into it. These groups also provide camaraderie as students navigate the often-turbulent waters of adolescence.

Small groups also matter because they promote intergenerational friendships and mentoring opportunities. The youth pastor cannot provide pastoral care for every single student. Even in a small ministry, some youth workers will bond with certain students better than the youth pastor can. Students need godly adults in their lives, in addition to their parents, who can model Christian maturity. When adults listen to students and genuinely care for them, great things happen.

WHAT HAPPENS IN A SMALL GROUP
- **Fun.** Opening with a game or activity isn't a waste of time. It helps create common ground among students while

setting the tone for how they should relate to each other. You cannot love one another if you cannot play or laugh together. This sets the tone for the rest of what happens in small groups.

- **Bible study.** This is the meaty portion of your time together. Generally, it is difficult to lead meaningful discussion in fewer than twenty minutes but students will rarely keep focused for more than forty-five. The best type of teaching in small groups is conversational and interactive. Prepare your lesson well, especially the questions you will ask.

- **Prayer.** Provide time for students to share prayer requests, but keep an eye on the clock. Sometimes students can talk for so long they don't actually have time to pray about what was shared. You may want to ask for a volunteer to pray as each request is shared, or you can have all the students share requests and then have a longer prayer time afterwards— but it's probably best to be consistent. Encourage and invite students to pray, but don't force them to pray out loud if they're uncomfortable.

- **Ministry development.** Training students to become leaders should be a part of every ministry's discipleship process. In small groups, this takes place by empowering students to assist (and then lead) parts of the group time. Small groups can also be an incredible way to mobilize students to reach their peers and community if they are given a vision and the skills necessary to dream, plan, and lead these projects.

BEST PRACTICES FOR SMALL GROUP LEADERS

- **Arrive early and well-prepared.** It will be difficult to welcome students if you are still setting up when they arrive. Be ready ten minutes prior to the meeting time.

- **Create a welcoming atmosphere.** You don't need to be the life of the party—just be yourself and genuinely care for the students in your group. If you do, they'll open up eventually.

- **Pray together.** For the first few weeks, you'll probably get a lot of prayer requests about school. Take note of what few details they give (science test, lots of homework, etc.) and follow up the next time you see them. That will show you're listening and genuinely care, and they'll slowly begin to share more.

- **Guard against sarcasm and gossip.** These can poison your group. Sarcasm gives the appearance of humor and informality, but it undermines genuine fellowship by keeping people at a safe distance by turning everything (even serious matters) into a joke. Gossip talks about people who are not present for the sake of entertainment. In a small group setting, this often happens when asking for prayer requests. Put a quick end to talking about those who are not present unless there is a genuine interest in coordinating efforts to serve and encourage them.

- **Let the gospel shape the way you correct bad behavior.** Youth ministry will always include some chaos. Care for students the way the Holy Spirit cares for your own sanctification: he convicts you of sin, invites you to repentance, and applies a heavy dose of grace.

- **Don't answer your own questions.** If you do, students will never answer because they know you'll bail them out. Instead, ask the question again in a different way. If there are co-leaders in the group, they should help each other by rewording the question.

How to Ask Good Questions

Bad questions are the main reason small groups struggle. Good leaders spend time thinking through their questions and writing them down ahead of time. They know those questions are the tools that lead either to fruitful discussions or to painful silences.

A bad question might be:

- So grand or vague it's hard even to know how to answer, especially if it's the first question. (Example: "How does it make you feel to know that God made you in his image?")

- So obvious it seems like a trick question. (Example: "What existed before God created the world?")
- One that sounds like the teacher is definitely looking for a certain answer—and you don't want to give the wrong one. (Example: "Why do you think it's important to know that God created people in his own image?")
- One that can be answered with a one-word response. (Example: "Who was the first person God created?")

Also vary the types of questions you ask throughout your lesson.

- **Content questions** can be answered by looking at the Scripture passage. They are objective, cut-and-dried questions. (Example: "In John 3:16, what does Jesus say is necessary for salvation?")
- **Reflection questions** help students process what they agree and disagree with in the passage. Where does this truth challenge or correct them? How does this make them feel? (Example: "When Jesus says 'You must be born again,' what does that imply about the relationship between our pre-Christian life and our post-Christian life?")
- **Application questions** consider how this shapes the head, heart, and hands. It is often easiest to ask an application question about a hypothetical peer before you ask students to apply it personally. (Example: "If your best friend became a Christian, what changes would you expect to see begin to take place in their life?")

27
Handling Discipline

It's safe to say that no one signed up to be a youth leader in order to discipline students when they misbehave. But these are incredibly important, teachable moments when we can apply the gospel. Sometimes, the things students do are so offensive they actually make us respond in ways that are sinful! But even when students are out of control, this is no excuse for us to lose our cool and sin against them in an effort to regain order.

So, how does the gospel shape our response when all we see is chaos? Grace doesn't replace discipline with unhindered permissiveness. The theological word for that is *antinomianism* (literally "no law"), and it's been regarded as heresy since the days of the early church. The gospel is not opposed to the law and to having clear rules and expectations. Instead, the gospel reframes how we treat the law.

In the same way that the law was given to show us our need for the Savior, a student's "lawbreaking" can show us that student's spiritual condition. When a genuinely converted student who broke the rules is invited to confess and repent, the student will do so. The gospel softens a believer's heart to correction. But students who habitually shift blame to others and refuse to take responsibility (and consequences!) for their behavior are showing you where they stand. They bristle and get angry. They roll their eyes and say they'll work on their behavior, but you both know they're going through the motions so you won't tell their parents—and students who do not respect human authority will also rebel against God's authority. For a ministry that values gospel repentance and discipleship, here are a few guardrails to have in place:

1. **Clarify expectations.** Without clear expectations, how are students supposed to know what kind of culture you are seeking to build in your ministry? Laying out what you expect students to do (and what they are not allowed to do) will paint a picture of the atmosphere you are seeking while also setting parameters for behavior. Repeat these expectations periodically to both students and their parents. Keep them short enough to be memorable, and reinforce them through affirmation and correction. Affirming and thanking students when they embody the culture you're cultivating (and being specific about what you saw them do) is powerful, and correcting behaviors that are contrary to your group atmosphere shows that you care enough about your expectations to uphold them.

2. **Embrace confession and accountability.** If your ministry is a place where students are publicly corrected and shamed, conversations to address behavior will become very difficult. Shame and guilt drive us to the shadows, not into the light. Grace, however, lets a potentially volatile conversations lead to repentance rather than merely being a reprimand. It is an opportunity for students to face their sinful pride and selfishness and also love their neighbor.

    This also applies to youth leaders, who should take responsibility for their own failures. If students have never heard us apologize for our failures when we've handled situations poorly, why should we expect students to respond with the humility we have failed to model? Ignoring bad behavior and neglecting discipline is pervasive in youth ministry and is often disguised as grace, but it is weak leadership that doesn't take its own rules seriously enough to enforce them.

3. **View discipline as an invitation.** Remember, your expectations should reflect the ministry culture you're trying to build and protect. Being intentional about this means that rather than yell at students ("Stop interrupting!") we encourage them to affirm each other's contributions ("What Billy is saying matters, Scott, and I'd like us all to hear what he has to say."). This invites students into the culture-building process of the ministry.

   The reality is that as soon as an adult yells, they've lost. The students are in control of that group—and they know it. Sometimes you will need to talk louder to get attention, but if you lose your head or yell often, you are in danger of shifting into a culture where youth leaders are policemen rather than shepherds. The tone and body language you take in the midst of discipline will largely determine how students respond.

4. **Graciously enforce consequences.** It is not wrong to ask a student not to attend youth group for a period of time. This type of consequence tells that student and the others that you are genuinely committed to building a certain culture in the youth group. Allowing troublemakers to consistently disrupt your ministry is not a service to the group. It's also not a service to those students, because you are implicitly teaching them that God doesn't care about their behavior and will not discipline those who disregard his commands.

   Of course, we should embrace grace. We should show patience, mercy, and kindness to students who struggle. There is a significant difference between a middle-school boy whose ADHD meds have worn off by youth group and an entitled teenager who finds joy in being disruptive. Students who come from difficult family backgrounds may require extra grace. This is why it is important to remember that discipline is part of the discipleship process. It is an opportunity to have a hard conversation with students and say, "I've noticed this behavior and have asked you to stop, but you haven't. Help me understand what's going on here. Because if it continues, there may be some discipline required to keep the group healthy so others don't start doing this too."

5. **Involve the parent(s).** Parents should be aware of the youth ministry's expectations. This makes talking about their student's bad behavior less tense and difficult. Whenever there is a hard conversation between a youth leader and a student, it's best for the parent to hear about that conversation directly from you. If you avoid parents, they will either assume everything is fine (because the student said nothing) or they will assume you are unfairly targeting their kid (because they're only hearing the student's perspective). In your conversation with the parent, be honest about what happened and what you said without embellishment or expressing frustration. Be clear-headed and calm. If you overreacted in the moment or said something you regret, have the integrity to admit it. That will earn you more trust and respect than you'll lose by ignoring what will be obvious to the parent.

If you claim you want to partner with parents in ministry to their kids but you are unwilling to discuss behavior problems with them, you're kidding yourself. This doesn't mean every parent should get a weekly behavior report. But if a student is causing problems in the group, the parent should know. Most parents want to be informed about their kids' behavior in the youth group. Take this opportunity to engage with parents as together you help their teenager develop a godly heart. Perhaps there's more going on in that student's life than you know, and a conversation with the parent will open up a meaningful collaboration for the student's benefit.

28
Using Social Media Effectively

Youth workers are often early adopters of new technology, and may be ahead of the curve in leveraging social media for meaningful ministry. Social media provides an additional way to connect with students and invest in them during the week. It is more than an efficient way to post announcements. When used well, it can heighten engagement with students, extend a sense of belonging in the group, and foster thoughtful reflection.

But there are dangers to consider. In addition to the negative impact social media can have on a student's mental health,[10] many youth workers have exchanged in-person time with students for time connecting with students through social media. Youth workers should remain able to repeat with the apostle Paul, "So, being affectionately desirous of you, we were ready to share with you not only the gospel of God but also our own selves, because you had become very dear to us" (1 Thessalonians 2:8). This posture toward students often leads youth workers to prayerfully use social media as an extension of their ministry, while being careful to not let it become a replacement for personal investment.

As life grows busier for both students and youth workers, the temptation to rely on social media and text messaging only increases. However, personal communication requires more than a screen can provide. Body language, tone, the pacing of speech, and the time it takes to know how to answer a question—these all get lost or significantly muted when conversations are mediated through technology. The intimacy of face-to-face conversations is likely the reason most teenagers actually prefer texting. But although teenagers are more likely to engage in a conversation that starts over texting or through social media, it is wise to look for ways to continue those conversations in person. It requires wisdom and self-restraint to leverage technology in a way that makes it a launchpad for relational discipleship, not a façade that looks like community but isn't the real thing.

SOCIAL MEDIA PITFALLS TO AVOID

- **Blurring the lines between youth workers and students.** Youth ministry can be a place for men and women who were outcasts during their own teen years to seek the affirmation and approval of today's teenagers. Most of the time, these youth workers do not even realize they are doing this. Other times, volunteers fall into using students to buffer their own insecurities, trying to appear cool and trendy in order to win students' favor. Certain social media platforms feed into this need to impress more than others. It is good for youth workers and students to have friendly relationships, but boundaries must be in place to prevent friendships from becoming codependent. These concern the youth worker's heart, and should be part of the interview process before a potential volunteer is invited to serve.
- **Displaying your own spiritual immaturity.** Youth workers should remember that their entire lives are a living example of mature Christianity to students. This includes their social media presence. If a youth worker is argumentative or self-absorbed or crass on social media, this is valid grounds for either terminating their leadership role or giving them

a break to put their spiritual life in order. Unchristian behavior online only teaches students that it's okay to be a different person at youth group than online.

- **Committing death by tech.** Death by tech happens when youth workers become so wrapped up in their digital presence that their actual time with students is limited to programs. Time is limited, and technology can easily give a sense of efficiency ("I've connected with six students this afternoon after school"). But a personal investment of time is far more significant. Taking students out for ice cream or sitting in the bleachers during a basketball game is far less efficient and can sometimes feel like a waste of an afternoon. But this is the type of sacrifice that shows students and parents that you care.

- **Only posting pictures with your favorite students.** When youth workers consistently share pictures of themselves hanging out with certain students, it can easily make others feel overlooked. Similarly, sharing pictures from sports events but not from musicals will communicate something about what types of students are a priority. This sort of favoritism (or perceived favoritism) can be deadly to a healthy youth-group culture, especially when it's done through the youth ministry's account as opposed to a leader's personal account. Since no one can be everywhere, collecting pictures from parents or other volunteers can ensure a wide array of students are celebrated and included. And a ministry where youth workers are careful to include students of all ethnicities from different school districts and with different interests has a powerful opportunity to celebrate all kinds of students and display the beauty of diversity within the body of Christ.

Social Media Best Practices

- **Think of social media as an airport.** No one goes to the airport for vacation. People go there in order to reach their destination. Social media should be treated similarly—not as an end in itself, but as an extension of personal relationships. If the coronavirus quarantine of 2020 taught youth workers anything, it's that technology and social media can have a truly helpful role when circumstances otherwise prevent connections. But it's entirely possible to overdo it. Conversations that take place online or through text messaging should be continued in person as much as possible.

- **Prioritize substance over style.** Resist the urge to curate your social media to make yourself relevant and compelling. Instead, seek true depth, and highlight that. This is at the core of the Christian's call to be counter-cultural. Dare to be different, because you are not competing with the world but rather holding out the invitation of the gospel. Use social-media platforms to encourage students to engage with Scripture, to think deeply, and to pray. Substance does not equal boring, so be engaging, fun, witty, and creative. But in all things, leave students with the Word of God and lead them into deeper faith.

- **Stay connected with students after graduation.** Among the greatest gifts social media has given is the ability to stay connected with students after they leave high school. Youth workers' relationships with graduates will change, naturally, but there will always be a certain level of respect as a spiritual authority. By sending occasional messages back and forth, it is possible to continue caring for these students as they navigate the next seasons of life.

- **Have clear guidelines for youth workers about what is appropriate.** Because every church and every ministry is different, it's wise for each team of youth workers to discuss social-media guidelines together. Whoever leads that conversation should also consult the church's child protection policy and seek counsel about how that document affects the ways that youth workers engage with students online. This may seem unnecessarily restrictive, but it is meant to allow youth workers to minister with clarity and with the safety of knowing they are covered by the collective wisdom of their team. Here are a few examples of good boundaries:

- Let parents know if small group leaders will be texting with their kids.
- Remember that students and their parents can see a leader's social-media accounts. Posting about alcohol and sex, or sharing crass jokes, is always a mistake and will diminish your credibility and trustworthiness as a youth worker.
- Male youth workers should avoid texting one-on-one messages to female students, and should include another female youth leader in the conversation as much as possible. Apps like GroupMe and WhatsApp keep a record of all conversations that can add an additional layer of security if any accusations arise.
- When youth leaders play video games with students online, they should honor parents' media limits and end games at a reasonable hour.

29

Thinking about LGBTQ Issues

N o handbook for today's youth workers would be complete
without offering guidance on ministry to students who
are either questioning their sexuality or have already embraced
an alternative lifestyle. A 2018 survey from the Barna Group
and Impact 360 reveals that 33 percent of teenagers believe a person's gender is determined by what the person feels like rather
than their birth sex.[11] Although only 3 percent of the American
population identifies as LGBTQ—lesbian, gay, bisexual, transgender, or queer—that number more than doubles to 7 percent
among teenagers. Additionally, 30 percent of teenagers know
someone who is transgender. The goal of this chapter is not
to present a defense of historic Christian sexuality, but to help
youth workers sensitively care for and minister to students in
these confusing times.

The rules for engaging students in a tolerant age (chapter
13) are essential: listen, repeat back, and keep the main thing
the main thing. This will help youth workers take a gracious
posture that covers a multitude of missteps and will assure
LGBTQ students that we are not their enemies. It is essential
to remember their greatest need is the same as the greatest need
of every student—to be reconciled with God through faith in
Jesus Christ.

Youth workers can trust the Word of God to do the work of God. The Bible has power to change people's hearts through the words God inspired. But Scripture is not a weapon to wield against sinners who need the grace of God. Youth workers build their ministries upon the Scriptures to proclaim the life and peace and hope of the gospel. In your ministry to LGBTQ students, pray for the Holy Spirit's illuminating work to turn the unbeliever's heart toward the truth.

Don't make every conversation with LGBTQ students about their sexuality, which would only anchor them deeper into viewing their sexuality as the most important thing about them. A focus on changing students' sexual orientation misses the bigger picture. The mission of youth ministry is not simply to make students' lives conform to godliness, because legalism can do that too (at least, on the surface). Instead, gospel-centered youth ministry calls students to live in light of the grace of Jesus Christ, confessing and repenting of their sins daily as they strive to live their new life in Christ through the power of the indwelling Holy Spirit.

LGBTQ IDENTITY

A key question is whether or not someone can embrace a homosexual or transgendered lifestyle and still be a Christian. A Christian's identity is first and foremost shaped by their relationship with God through Jesus Christ, so I am uncomfortable with combining any other adjective with the label *Christian*. When we do that, there is a subtle competition between the two identities. The Christian's identity as a Christian should be the core identity that reshapes and refines every other identifier: gender, nationality, sexuality, cultural preferences, denominational affiliations, etc. These other identifiers may be valid and important, but they must be shaped by God and by the authority of Scripture rather than the other way around. The Bible does not permit homosexual activity, and it teaches us that a person's sex and gender are assigned by our wise and loving God at birth.

Christians who live with gender dysphoria or same-sex attraction embrace their identity in Christ as their primary identity rather than allowing their sexuality to be the most important thing about them. This is often a confusing and difficult road for them, and youth workers are called to ensure they don't walk it alone.

The call of the gospel is an invitation to a new life through grace-fueled repentance. A new believer will not repent of every sin immediately; it is a lifelong journey that requires much grace (from God and from others!). But Christians do repent eventually. The Holy Spirit is at work in their hearts, persuading them of the goodness and truthfulness of God's Word—even when it brings conviction of sin. Those who profess faith in Christ Jesus but never repent of sin show that, although they may be trying to gain the treasures of heaven, they do not really want new life as a child of God. The timeline for this repentance may take years because of the nature of sexual confusions—be generous in longsuffering with students and LGBTQ friends. If a practicing homosexual or transgendered person professes to be a Christian and yet persists in rejecting the Bible's teaching on sexuality, that person's conversion remains questionable.

But rather than lobbing this warning as a grenade, offer concern that befits the gospel. It is not a cop-out to leave judgment in God's hands. The Lord has not rushed into judgment, and neither should youth workers. So when in doubt, err on the side of patience. At the same time, Christian leaders will be held accountable for holding fast to biblical teaching (James 3:1), and it is not loving or gracious to affirm a professing Christian's sinful lifestyle, regardless of what that particular sin may be.

COMMON TERMS AND LABELS

One of the easiest ways for youth workers to discredit themselves when discussing LGBTQ with students is to demonstrate ignorance about how LGBTQ advocates define and use their words. Here are some of the more common terms every youth worker should know:

- Sex: The biological and hormonal makeup of a person, assigned at birth.
- Gender: The social constructs that describe acceptable behavior for the sexes.
- Cisgender: A person who exclusively identifies as their birth gender.
- Nonbinary: Those whose gender is not easily categorized as male or female, sometimes a broader label for asexual, queer, or transgendered persons.
- Gender dysphoria: A clinical condition where a person suffers distress because their sex and gender identity are in conflict.
- Gender identity: A person's internal and innate sense of gender, which may or may not align with their sex.
- Sexual orientation: A person's expression of romantic and sexual longing. LGBTQ advocates tie orientation to gender identity, not to sex. Thus, they consider a transgendered woman whose orientation leads to relationships with women a lesbian.

LGBTQ Practical Considerations

1. **Gender pronouns.** For the sake of pastoral care and compassion, it is usually best to use students' preferred pronouns. This is likely a church-by-church decision and is best made in consultation with the senior pastor and elders or deacons of your church. Refusing to use students' preferred pronouns will likely eliminate any potential ministry or evangelism to LGBTQ students (and perhaps their friends also).
2. **Bathrooms.** If you have a transgendered student in your ministry, it is likely they are stressed about what bathroom they should use and routinely avoid using public bathrooms whenever possible. It would be ideal to have a private

conversation with that student and one of their parents, in person, to discuss how you can best provide for their needs. This will cultivate trust because you are compassionately addressing a difficult topic head-on while also building clear expectations.

3. **Small Groups.** Dividing small groups according to gender is the default model for most ministries, but it puts those who are struggling with their gender identity in a difficult place. Placing transgender students in a gender-based small group for their birth-sex will cause them great anxiety, while including them in the group according to their gender identity will place the spotlight on them in some uncomfortable ways (especially if they grew up in the church with those other boys or girls). Instead, consider restructuring small groups to be co-ed, while hosting occasional events for high school boys or girls. If you choose to not restructure all small groups, it is highly recommended to have one or two co-ed groups as an option.

4. **Housing during retreats.** This is likely your most difficult decision, and you should make it in consultation with the leadership of your church after you have contacted the camp or retreat center to learn your options. Chances are, you are not the first youth worker to call with this question, and the retreat staff may have suggestions. If your retreat is discipleship oriented, this student's interest in attending may open a difficult but fruitful conversation about their relationship with Christ. If it's a more evangelistic retreat, putting in extra work to accommodate the student's attendance may prove fruitful. If the student is not able to attend, or is too uncomfortable to *want* to attend, then remember that the same Holy Spirit who works at retreats also works through your regular ministry.

5. **Coarse joking and mockery.** When other students make jokes about gender or orientation, it is a deep wound upon those who are struggling with their secret battles. Cultivating *and guarding* an atmosphere of welcome and love is of the

utmost importance. This is not a compromise with God's holy standards, but an expression of compassion to students who are coming to your ministry hoping to be loved in the midst of their anxieties and uncertainties. When a student thoughtlessly makes a crude joke and is corrected with a dismissive, "C'mon Johnny, knock it off," the group can see that it's not a big deal—and those comments will continue. It is never right to shame a student, so don't be too harsh, but respond with equal measures of grace and firmness, "Johnny, I don't appreciate that. We don't do that here."

6. **Ministry plan.** Does the student profess to be a Christian? This is the most important question to consider when determining your ministry plan to LGBTQ students. It is foolish to hold non-Christians to biblical standards. Christians need discipleship, but unbelievers need evangelism. The gospel must be front-and-center in both approaches, but identifying where the student is in their relationship with Christ is the first question to consider when determining your response. As the common observation goes, if you have met one LGBTQ student, you have only met one LGBTQ student. Their backgrounds and current needs are different from each other. Develop a posture toward all LGBTQ students, but build your ministry plan according to each individual.

FURTHER READING

Kevin DeYoung, *What Does the Bible Really Teach about Homosexuality?* (Wheaton, IL: Crossway, 2015).

Jackie Hill Perry, *Gay Girl, Good God: The Story of Who I Was, and Who God Has Always Been* (Nashville, TN: B&H Publishing, 2018).

Abigail Shrier, *Irreversible Damage: The Transgender Craze Seducing Our Daughters* (Washington, D.C.: Regnery Publishing, 2020).

Andrew T. Walker, *God and the Transgender Debate: What Does the Bible Actually Say about Gender-Identity?* (Charlotte, NC: The Good Book Company, 2017).

Evangelical Alliance, *Trans Formed: A Brief Biblical and Pastoral Introduction to Understanding Transgender in a Changing Culture* (London, UK: Evangelical Alliance, 2018) Accessed 11/20/20, https://www.eauk.org/assets/files/downloads/Transformed.pdf.

30

Helping Students Who Struggle with Porn

Youth workers cannot offer parents "three keys to porn-proof your kid." Pornography is fundamentally a heart issue. When parents discover their son or daughter has been viewing it, their first and understandable reaction is to freak out. This makes sense; especially when we consider that the average age of first exposure to pornography happens during the middle-school years or before.[12] Although most initial exposures are accidental—an innocent misspelling of a popular website, or a click on a link they did not realize would lead to a dark corner of the internet—every parent hopes their son or daughter will avoid the snare of pornography. They need to know they are not alone in struggling with how to navigate the porn talk with their child.

Talking about pornography use with students is one of the trickier elements of youth ministry. Parents need to take the lead in ongoing conversations about all areas of sexuality with their teenagers. Youth workers should see themselves as allies who come alongside the parents to help their teenager develop a biblical view of sexuality. Your mention of porn use could easily come across as accusatory, guaranteeing the student will never confess such a sin to you. At the same time, avoiding this difficult topic can lead a student to feel like their shame must remain hidden.

Addressing the Heart

The heart of porn is dissatisfaction. Accountability groups, tracking or filtering software, or getting rid of students' smartphones may be helpful. But only the gospel truly delivers from false gods and sinful addictions. No one becomes holier by being told, "Just stop sinning and be more like Jesus." This is why parents and youth workers need to do the work necessary to address the heart, not only the behavior.

An alarming number of students turn to porn for stress relief and comfort when life is challenging or sad. With porn, they will never face rejection and will be able to vicariously live out fantasies they would never actually pursue in real life. But this illusion of power and desirability is not without consequence. Students' dissatisfaction with themselves and with the world can easily trap them in the clutches of a long-standing and destructive porn habit that leaves them feeling hollow inside.

Porn promises satisfaction, but porn is a liar. It cannot deliver true satisfaction that dispels the emptiness that drives students to porn in the first place. Only Jesus can do that. When students discover the beauty and grace of Jesus Christ, it's a game changer. Because Jesus took our sins on the cross, all our guilt and shame (including private sexual sins) has been atoned for. In its place, we receive joy and peace and love—not temporary joy, but everlasting contentment and fulfillment in the presence of God. An ongoing porn habit numbs that divine joy with a cheap imitation.

The best thing parents and youth workers can do is to keep proclaiming the beauty and grace of Jesus Christ in the gospel—and let their own lives put that joy on display. Helping students behold Christ crucified, risen, ascended, and coming again is the best way to defeat any sin, pornography included.

What Porn Does to Students

An increasing number of secular researchers have sounded the alarm about the negative effects of porn on the brain. Neural pathways that trigger addiction form in the brain with great speed and intensity while consuming porn, and these pathways overpower more important human needs. The brain gets used to certain triggers that make it crave an increasing amount of porn while also emitting addictive hormones. Pleasure sensors in the brain respond to porn in ways that are shockingly similar to a heroin addict's brain. There is a need to consume an increasing amount of porn to be satisfied.

Porn addicts are often burdened by shame even as they begin to sexualize the people in their lives. Pornography not only burns images into students' brains, it has become the de facto sex education for many teenagers. It answers the questions they are too embarrassed to ask and shows them how to give and receive pleasure. Surely, this is cause for great alarm.

For teenagers, whose brains are still developing and whose bodies are in the midst of significant change, this is dangerous territory. And yet, porn use among teenagers is at epidemic levels, and it is not merely a guy problem. Although teen boys consume more porn than girls do, it is not uncommon for girls also to swim in the murky waters of pornography. Interestingly, it is a rare topic that is both shameless (because "everyone's doing it" and supposedly it isn't harming anyone) and deeply shameful (we just don't talk about it, especially with adults).

Helping Parents Help Their Kids

Parents and youth workers should be on the same page regarding pornography, including the parents' primary role in these conversations. Highlighting the grace of Christ that removes our shame is important, because many fathers are either in the throes of porn use themselves or refuse to talk about it with their kids because of their shame, while mothers can easily see it as "gross" and something their kids should simply choose not to do anymore. How you lead these conversations with parents will give them a roadmap for how they can discuss sensitive issues with their kids.

Providing semi-regular roundtable forums for parents will provide a healthy setting to equip them to take the lead in discussing sexuality with their kids. Encourage parents to be discreet about their child's privacy, but allow them freedom to ask difficult questions in a safe setting with a few other parents. This will allow them to respond with greater composure and helpfulness than if they had never given any thought to how they will discuss this topic with their teenager. Role-playing these difficult conversations might help nervous parents become more confident.

Also help parents find good resources and filters for their internet. It is wise to have time and app limitations for students, especially when they are younger. Still, anyone who wants to find porn online can work diligently enough to find a way, so filters are not solutions, but signposts for students that say, "You have to work this much to get around the filter for a reason. Reconsider whether or not you *really* want to do this. Choose holiness and integrity instead. You won't be disappointed." Filters cannot fix a student's heart, but needing to jump through the extra hoops to view porn can provide the reminder the student needs to resist temptation.

Many parents are lulled into inaction by assuming the internet filters will reshape their children's hearts into the image of Christ. If the only response to porn is to add filters and stop the student from viewing it again, the underlying cravings of the flesh will find another outlet. Ministering to students who struggle with porn must involve digging into the heart issues that are driving this sinful habit. Pornography is a symptom of a larger craving in the students' life that parents and youth workers will want to address.

The best thing a youth worker can do to support parents whose teen has been watching porn is to remind them of the beauty and satisfaction of the gospel. Every Christian has been called out of sin and into the light. Now that their teen's sin has been unveiled, shine the light of Jesus onto it. Show it for what it is: a delusion that porn satisfies better than Jesus, a belief that other people's bodies are a means to our own pleasure, and a complicit participation in human trafficking and rape that has been captured on video and shared on the internet for viewers' enjoyment. Not only that, but students are sinning against their own bodies as they damage their neural pathways, fuel addictions in the brain's pleasure center, and possibly even create sexual dysfunction that will creep into their future marriage.

If the student is a professing Christian, they have been justified by the blood of Jesus Christ, and this is an opportunity for sanctification. Parents should not place the burden of guilt and shame back onto their teenager, hoping it might motivate them to escape porn's grip in the future. Such a burden will likely only drive the student into deeper shame and secrecy. The grace of God means the guilt and shame is already forgiven, and now confession and holiness are theirs by faith in Jesus. Let this be the context for discussing pornography and sexual sin.

31

Discussing Sex and Dating

S ex is like fire. When it resides in the proper boundaries it gives light and heat, but unrestrained it causes great harm. Teenagers are receiving messages about sexuality every day—from the latest Netflix series, from social media, from their conversations with friends. Parents and youth workers must not overlook the value of having their own ongoing conversations with students about biblical sexuality.

Youth ministry has a legacy of urging teenagers to make "virginity pledges" and other similar efforts that can easily drift into manipulation. While the intent is good, since we should be teaching about sexual purity, the way we engage in these conversations matters. By now it should be obvious that we need to talk about sex in light of the gospel of Jesus Christ, not according to the law. It is not a matter of dos and don'ts but of helping students discover the nature of sex, the goal of sex, and the fulfillment of what sex can offer.

When youth group only talks about sex once a year, usually a few weeks before prom season, it makes sense that many students will be more shaped by the messages the culture and their peers are sending: "Sex is awesome." "Love is love." "Be careful, but do what you want so long as the other person gives consent." Others graduate from youth ministry with the impression that sex is inherently sinful. Some Christians even feel guilty about having sex after they get married because of the way sex was discussed during their teen years. The solution is not to overcorrect by talking about how great and awesome sex is, but simply to be biblical.

God created gender, sex, and marriage to promote human flourishing. He did not need to make it feel good, but he did. It is a gift that reflects the delight and pleasure we were created to enjoy through intimacy with our Creator. At the same time, the Bible doesn't pull punches about the dangers of unbounded sexuality. The cities of Sodom and Gomorrah were destroyed as judgment for their rampant evil and sexuality. King David, a man after God's own heart, caused great suffering in his family because of his sexual sin against Bathsheba.

Sex Is a Quest for Intimacy

God gave the gift of sex to strengthen intimacy between a husband and a wife. The goal is intimacy—to be fully known without any fear of rejection. This is what so many men and women are trying to attain through their sexual activity, as if sex were a shortcut to it. Whether we are talking with parents or students, it is helpful and biblical to build the conversation around intimacy: God created us for intimacy with him and with each other. Sin has brought suspicion into relationships, but sex is a brief moment of joyful acceptance between two partners. Aside from the physical pleasure, this is what makes it so powerful.

This quest for intimacy also gives fulfillment to men and women who never marry. To many students, the idea of singleness can sound like a sentence to lifelong loneliness, and this fear drives them into toxic dating patterns. However, celibacy is an old-fashioned virtue worth reclaiming, especially considering that neither Jesus nor the apostle Paul ever married. Some churches treat married couples and those with children as priority members, but this should not be, and youth workers have an opportunity to teach students a wider view of human sexuality and relationships.

Sex is about intimacy, and perfect intimacy is found only in Jesus Christ who loved us and saved us while we were still enemies. God chose to redeem sinners and adopt them as sons and daughters. If he gave his life for us while we were still his enemies, then truly nothing can separate us from the love of God. In the midst of today's sexual revolution, it is important to remember that sex is about enjoying intimacy with a spouse and yet, as good as sex may feel, it cannot deliver the type of intimacy our hearts most desire.

BEST PRACTICES FOR DISCUSSING SEX AND DATING

- **Always talk with parents first.** Whether you are teaching in youth group or initiating a conversation with a student at the coffee shop, always talk with parents first. Many youth workers have assumed parents would be comfortable with another adult having these conversations with their kids, only to find out they were wrong. Plus, if the talk goes sideways, you'll be thankful to have parental support while dealing with the fallout.
- **Make it an ongoing conversation.** As you preach through biblical texts, make ongoing applications to students' dating lives and sexual identities. If the only time you talk about sex is when the entire lesson is about sex, you're missing a chance to shape the whole person.
- **Avoid a lot of joking about who's dating whom.** Laughter is good medicine, but it can also make having serious conversations awkward. Students may become hesitant to ask you about relationships because they fear you might turn it into a joke.
- **Teach about a biblical view of marriage.** It can be tempting to avoid talking about marriage because teenagers are likely not getting married anytime soon. Inviting married couples of various ages to share their stories and what they've learned about marriage can be especially helpful for students from fractured households, because they may not receive this type of teaching (or example!) anywhere else.

- **Don't overlook the Bible's teaching about celibacy.** Christian men and women who never marry are just as important and valuable as those who have large families. Especially in today's climate surrounding LGBTQ identities, reclaiming the holiness of celibacy enables students to hear that it is possible to be both celibate and fulfilled in life.
- **Avoid damaging illustrations and examples.** Many skits and examples have been used in youth ministry to persuade students about sexual abstinence. The most popular has been handing out a piece of gum for someone to chew, only to later hold up the piece of chewed gum and ask "Who wants this?" This illustration and others like it implicitly tell students who have sinned sexually that they are worthless and undesirable, both to other people and to God. The gospel, however, proclaims the love of God for sinners and his delight in giving grace to those who need it.
- **Resist talking about "sexual purity until marriage."** Married men and women also need to guard their sexual purity. When youth workers talk about sexual purity *until* marriage, this either conveys that sex with your spouse makes you impure or that you will not need to guard yourself against sexual sin after marriage. Rather than making it seem like sexual purity is a teenage problem, call students to sexual purity as a lifelong pursuit.
- **Consider speaking to the boys and girls separately.** There are times when large-group teaching may be best, but consider ways to speak to students in forums that will minimize awkward moments while maximizing the potential for real conversation.
- **Ask students about their friends' views.** This will allow them to talk with greater comfort. It will also help you interact with the other viewpoints they're hearing and get a glimpse of their own opinions. How you respond to this conversation will help them decide whether or not they can trust you.

- **Keep the grace of Jesus Christ front-and-center.** Sex is about intimacy, and perfect intimacy is found through fellowship with God in Christ.

32

Organizing a Ministry Calendar

Leading a youth ministry is about more than the programs on the calendar, but those events do have significance. They contribute toward students' maturity in Christ, so it is worth taking the time to organize and lead them well. After all, if no one shows up or if they do show up but it's a train wreck, they won't show up next time—and why should they?

How to Decide Which Events to Do

- **Emphasize your priorities.** It will be tempting either to look at your strengths and build on those or to look at the ministry's weaknesses and seek to address them through special programming. Although this seems wise, it's actually counterproductive. Instead, think bigger. Consider the overall mission and priority of the ministry, and then ask how an event can make progress toward fulfilling that vision. By moving in the direction of the ministry's priorities, every area of the ministry gets pulled into healthier alignment.
- **Have a clear discipleship map.** If all ministry programs are listed on a whiteboard, it should be possible to plug hypothetical students into the ministry and watch them progress in spiritual maturity. Evangelism is central, but if

every program is for non-believers or new believers, where will students grow deep roots in faith? Discipleship is essential, but if there is nowhere for disciples to invite their friends, how are we helping students evangelize? Fun events are wonderful for building community, but it is easy to invest so much in them that little is left for discipleship. And service projects are among the most overlooked discipleship opportunities—an excellent way for students to observe and practice servant-leadership. All of these programs have value for making disciples, but they can end up simply keeping you busy unless you've formed a clear discipleship plan. Planning the youth ministry calendar is one of the most important elements of leading students to Jesus. It is where the ministry's true priorities are reflected, because you need to decide what to do and what good opportunities to say no to. Making hard decisions to reduce the number of events so you can build a sustainable discipleship plan can be painful but is worth it.

- **Foster a healthy group culture.** Discipleship doesn't happen in a vacuum. A ministry's discipleship map should incorporate various kinds of lived experiences that show students what the Christian life looks like—in good times and in bad, while rejoicing and while sharing in grief. These can include service projects, mission trips, camps, or something as simple as a night at the bowling alley. Frame these experience-driven events so that their purpose is clear and student leaders are empowered to lead by example.

- **Evaluate the cost and benefit.** Sometimes leaders need to admit they simply do not have the time, budget, or manpower to pull off a highly-desired event. Every youth worker will experience events that, in hindsight, were loads of fun but didn't seem to make much impact, while other events that were extremely simple proved surprisingly effective. Bigger isn't always better. Sometimes a simple event is exactly what's needed. The easiest way to conduct a cost/benefit analysis of an event is to make a list of all the required resources to make it successful (people, time, budget, student buy-in) followed by a list of those same resources that are readily available. The wider the gap, the more an event "costs." And the more it costs, the more it needs to directly feed into the ministry's discipleship map. High-cost events that are loosely aligned with student discipleship should either be canceled or reconfigured to better fit ministry priorities—else they will, in time, *become* the ministry's functional priority.

How to Plan and Run an Event

1. Keep your mission in front of you. Refuse to add elements that don't contribute to the goal, even if they're super fun, because they can overtake the purpose of your program.
2. Map out what the event would look like in an ideal world. Dream about how it could make a significant impact.
3. Conduct your cost/benefit analysis. Discover the cost of doing the event the ideal way.
4. Adjust your plan, accounting for the cost and benefit while keeping your mission and ministry priorities in place.
5. Make a schedule for the event. Plan backward from the end time. (This might be the most valuable piece of practical advice in this chapter: determine your end-time, and then schedule backward.)
6. Recruit help, especially from parents and students.
7. Work with student leaders to make final adjustments to the plan and to promote the event.
8. Assign roles and tasks to volunteers ahead of time, with specific instructions and all materials provided. This should free the primary leader from any busywork and important but menial tasks. Small group leaders and other regular youth workers should be able to spend time ministering to students during the event while "special agents" fill other volunteer roles.
9. During the event, keep instructions and announcements brief by rehearsing them multiple times before students

arrive. The primary leader should be free to direct the overall program to address bigger problems while other volunteers solve problems specific to their tasks.

10. Within two weeks after the event, evaluate and debrief as a team. Create a document for each leader to list their observations under the following categories: Keep, Change, Drop, Add. Compile the evaluations and file them for future use.

33

How to Plan a Mission Trip

Mission trips can be among the most life-changing experiences in a student's life before graduation. Often, their eyes and hearts are uniquely opened to finally see needs they have otherwise been blind to. For some, it may be their first time learning the names of men and women and children whose lives are marked by poverty, addiction, and other issues that usually remain distant and faceless because of students' privilege.

Planning a short-term mission trip requires forethought, wisdom, and steady leadership. Good planning will maximize the benefit for both your hosting ministry and your team.

Short-term mission trips are biblical. The Bible clearly teaches about the importance of global missions. In the Great Commission, Jesus sends his apostles to "make disciples of all nations" (Matthew 28:19). Before he ascends into glory, Jesus tells them, "You will be my witnesses in Jerusalem and in all Judea and Samaria, and to the end of the earth" (Acts 1:8). The gospel is for all people everywhere. But what place does a short-term team of students play in this global mission?

The Gospels mention two instances when Jesus sent out short-term mission teams. In Matthew 10:5–15, he sent the twelve apostles to preach the kingdom of God and to perform signs and wonders attesting to their message. And in Luke 10:1–12, he sent groups of other disciples to villages he would soon be visiting. It would be difficult to make a hard argument that these texts make a pattern for all short-term mission trips, but they do present biblical examples of effective short-term ministry. They show us the value of sending disciples out to do ministry.

SELECTING A SHORT-TERM MISSION FOR LONG-TERM IMPACT

There has been much discussion over the last decade about the harm that short-term mission teams can bring to a community. Sometimes, overseeing their work can tax the long-term leaders whose ministry is disrupted so they can direct the visiting team. Other times, teams raise a significant amount of money to do work that local workers could do for a fraction of the cost. There are also cycles of dependency that run deep within certain communities, leading the locals to view themselves as reliant on those who come to help. In the worst of cases, the sending churches go to serve with pity more than love. But healthy short-term teams serve the needy with compassion while giving them genuine dignity and contributing to the ministry of long-term workers.

If the church supports full-time missionaries, sending short-term teams can be a fruitful way to deepen those partnerships. Done poorly, short-term mission teams pull the long-term workers from their regular ministries in order to babysit their guests, so it is important to be open and gracious in those first conversations to ensure the team will legitimately contribute to the ministry. But a short-term team that works with the long-term workers to extend their normal capacity is a wonderful blessing to the church.

Be highly selective when serving alongside a short-term mission organization that runs trips for youth groups. This will help you avoid situations where gospel disagreements take place mid-trip with the organization's leaders. Youth ministry mission trips have a tendency to emphasize work projects (like disaster relief), social justice issues (feeding the homeless), or children's ministry (run a vacation Bible school). These can be very good ways to help those in need while giving students a vision for loving their neighbor, but these projects are often light on direct gospel ministry. It is imperative to keep the gospel central in all mission work, even if the projects are primarily physical labor rather than direct evangelism. Otherwise, the difference between a mission trip and a service trip is negligible. If students can go on a mission trip without having a conversation about Jesus, something is wrong. Address this directly when vetting mission organizations.

PRACTICAL COUNSEL FOR LEADING A YOUTH TEAM

Before you go . . .

- Determine your team's ministry objectives. If you want students to develop a heart for the homeless and open their eyes to systemic injustice, you will plan a very different trip than if your primary objective is evangelism training. This also impacts which students should be eligible to participate.
- Choose ministry partners who share your gospel convictions and have a track record of making a long-term investment in a ministry area that fits your objectives.
- Determine the financial cost. Consider airfare, vehicle rentals and gasoline, housing, food, ministry materials, team-building and planning, and the organization's fee. It helps to factor in an additional 5 percent for each student to ensure that surprise expenses will be covered. In some cases of international travel, there will be passport fees and other added expenses. Adults who participate as leaders will often ask if they are expected to pay the same price as students. It's wise to have a regular policy instead of changing your approach each year.
- Contact the ministry partner to send your deposit and finalize plans by Thanksgiving, roughly nine months before a summer mission trip. Many youth mission organizations will be at capacity if you wait until January. You should have a basic plan in place by Thanksgiving. Students don't have to apply that early, but you need to commit as an organization and start planning.
- Make a form or brochure for students and parents that presents essential information: ministry objective, location,

dates, cost, requirements, housing (including the availability of showers), and the application deadline. Along with an informational brochure, create an application form to collect students' basic information, their testimony, why they want to serve on the team, and what strengths they bring. About a month before the sign-up deadline, host an informational meeting to answer remaining questions.

- Create a partnership with parents, students, and leaders to raise funds for team expenses. Delegating others to lead this effort will save you considerable time and empowers them to contribute to the ministry.

- Prepare the team to serve. There should be three or four team meetings in the months prior to the trip. These orient the team to go as servant-leaders, give students roles and responsibilities within the team, and build some team chemistry before the mission trip. Participate in at least one service project during this time so students can serve together before the trip.

During the trip . . .

- Begin each day with time in Scripture and prayer. Some teams will have a student or adult lead a devotional for the team followed by small-group prayer. Others will have devotional guides for individuals to read on their own, and then gather for discussion and prayer afterward. Use this time to teach and model for students how to devotionally read the Bible.

- Have a regular check-in each morning and evening for adult leaders. This will enable them to be well-informed so they can lead during the day without extensive oversight.

- Debrief each day with the team, but keep it fairly short since everyone will likely be tired. Invite students to share a daily high and daily low, which lets you take the pulse of the team dynamics and each individual. Discuss the team's victories of the day and identify one or two specific ways your team will improve tomorrow.

- Address conflict directly, but with grace. Model biblical conflict resolution by talking with the people involved before bringing the matter before the team, which should only be done in extreme circumstances. It will be helpful to discuss healthy conflict resolution during a pre-trip meeting, since this is frequently one of the greatest challenges a team will face. Although conflict can breed division in a group, it also provides the greatest teachable moments when you can apply the gospel to students' experiences.
- Keep a positive spirit in the midst of changes. Every mission trip will include a change of plans along the way—hopefully nothing major, but changes are normal. If the leader gets frustrated or discouraged, the team will respond similarly. Asking good questions while remaining optimistic will make you a good example to students.
- Restrain sarcasm and gossip. These quickly destroy a mission team. There can be no unity if team members are guarded with each other due to a lack of trust and respect.

After the trip . . .
- Within two weeks after returning, debrief the adult volunteers. Discuss the strengths and weaknesses of the team's experience and whether or not the primary mission of the team was fulfilled. Together, craft some good questions to ask when you meet with the students.
- Host a celebration for the entire team three to five weeks after returning. This is long enough removed that some of the emotions have waned but the lessons are still fresh. As you celebrate highlights and memories, discuss how you can share those lessons with the youth group and with the whole church.
- If possible, a great ministry opportunity is for the students to make a presentation to the church family during a worship service, Sunday school, or special evening. This lets students share what they've learned with the church, and lets the church support students' spiritual development.

34

Navigating Conflict Between Students

Drama. It comes with the territory of youth ministry. Whether it's over something that makes you roll your eyes or something that is legitimately sinful, it is a ministry moment between youth workers and students that can provide a rich opportunity to teach and apply the gospel to real life. A healthy group culture doesn't mean there is no conflict; it means conflict is addressed with honestly and with grace.

The gospel is a message of peace for those who were living in conflict with God. As Paul explains, "God shows his love for us in that while we were still sinners, Christ died for us" (Romans 5:8). Because the gospel itself is a message of reconciliation between God and people, we are instructed, "Be kind to one another, tenderhearted, forgiving one another, as God in Christ forgave you" (Ephesians 4:32). Forgiving others begins by remembering the mercy and grace you have received through Jesus Christ.

Peacemaking is intrinsic to the gospel. Jesus taught his disciples, "Love your enemies and pray for those who persecute you" (Matthew 5:44). Gospel people should be peacemakers, whether they are the offender or the offended, or a concerned friend who wants to mediate reconciliation.

It is easy to talk about peacemaking as if it's merely a choice: "Just choose to forgive." But true peacemaking acknowledges the severity of the offense while leaning into a posture of forgiveness and reconciliation. Forgiveness requires the offended party to face the pain while choosing to let it go, to show the mercy and grace God has given through Jesus Christ. The gospel empowers forgiveness.

UNHEALTHY CONFLICT RESOLUTION

One of the unexpected roles of a youth pastor is that of mediator. Whether the conflict is between students, parents, or leaders, there are a few common ways people react. The responses below are only a few. For an excellent treatment of this topic, see Ken Sande's book, *The Peacemaker*.[13]

Avoiding. This may be the most common response to conflict from teenagers. In your effort to help, be careful to not assume the worst. Maybe the student was hurt in the moment and is legitimately able to overlook the offense without any bitterness or resentment. But when students are avoiding the conflict, hurt and bitterness will be hiding under the veil of pretending everything is fine. Without becoming accusatory, youth workers will want to help students admit the pain they are experiencing and navigate what it will look like to seek healing, forgiveness, and reconciliation rather than "stuffing it."

Attacking. Some students' disposition is set to attack mode. They rarely take correction well and they have a high passion for justice (especially when they've been wronged). Resist the urge to fight back. Instead, de-escalate the anger by responding with compassion and understanding. When handled poorly, students in attack mode can wound many in the group and create more conflict. Even when the offense that angered them is legitimate, it is a pastoral moment to direct these angry students to the cross where God's perfect justice and mercy are on display. Serving as an agent of reconciliation is an important piece of student ministry.

Passive-aggressiveness. When students respond passive-aggressively, they exchange angry outbursts for the slow drip of bitterness. This usually comes out through sarcasm, mockery, and demeaning nonverbals at the other person's expense. A common expression of this in youth culture is "throwing shade," jokingly criticizing another person in a way that is funny but hurtful. Youth workers will want to help students see how this posture only deepens the rift between parties and does nothing to promote reconciliation.

Gossiping. Gossip is saying something behind someone's back that you'd never say to their face. Another helpful definition could be, "Talking negatively about someone without any intention to help." Gossip often involves telling the truth. But gossip spreads information that assassinates another person's character and trustworthiness. Usually, this is done to strengthen opposition against the other person in order to build allegiances. A peacemaking response to conflict resists both gossip and lies, instead taking the hard road toward restoration.

PEACEMAKING IN YOUTH MINISTRY

The following is not necessarily step-by-step instructions, but a list of observations and hard-learned counsel that will help you grow as a peacemaking youth worker.

Get first-hand information. Don't rely on what others tell you. This is especially true when the conflict arose through social media, where gossip spreads so quickly. You may be tempted to avoid approaching the students involved in order to protect those who told you about the conflict. But although you should practice wisdom and discretion, it is good to talk with those involved—because you genuinely care about the conflict being resolved. Be careful before making promises of confidentiality. And if you have made such a promise, let the person who confided in you know that you feel the need to act on the information you have received *before* you do it.

Resist the temptation to become a busybody. Don't insert yourself into situations where you don't belong. But when students have sinned against one another, there may be a legitimate pastoral concern to address.

Be wise about when and how to initiate hard conversations. Patience really is a virtue. Don't be hasty in talking with students about conflict. However, do not allow patience and carefulness to become complacency that allows conflict to remain unaddressed.

Partnering with parents means you should keep them informed. This is a widely-debated matter among youth workers. But if you truly want to partner with parents, and if conflict provides some of the greatest teachable moments, then it is wise to inform parents of conflicts. This is especially true if a conflict is causing division and hurt feelings among other students. Besides, there is a strong chance the parent is already aware that something has happened. You do not need to tell everything about the conflict, but inviting parents into the process can help you understand contributing factors you may not have known about.

If you cannot be objective, find someone who can. Perhaps the conflict involves a student with whom you are particularly close, or with whom you have a strained relationship. Then it may be best to find another wise and godly adult who can stand in the gap as a peacemaker.

You are not the accuser. You are also not the judge, deciding who is right and wrong. On those occasions when there is a very clear case of abuse that has been committed, pray for wisdom and self-control to mediate the conversation. Speak honestly and directly with students, but with a heavy dose of empathy and mercy. Allow the Holy Spirit to convict students of their sin and their contribution to the conflict. Realize that this probably will not happen through a single conversation, but over time.

Get to the heart. It is possible to walk through the entire reconciliation process and achieve fake peace because the heart issues were never addressed. Listen carefully to what is not being said and ask thoughtful questions to help students uncover the reasons they said, felt, or behaved the way they did.

Forgiveness can be a long and difficult journey. Christians don't pretend the offense never happened. Instead, forgiveness means the conflict has been replaced by a willingness to rebuild trust over time.

35

Breaking Down Cliques

All youth workers believe their group has a problem with cliques. Talking about cliques with students is a challenge because some (usually those on the outside) would report cliques as the greatest danger in the youth ministry while others (usually students who are in a clique) believe they don't exist. The solution is not to forbid close friendships, but to cast a vision for true unity.

Most churches draw worshipers from multiple towns, often from as far as half an hour away. This means students have grown up in rival schools where they've been trained to crush, destroy, and annihilate each other since childhood. It's no surprise then that some divisions will stem from town or school allegiances. Other times, cliques can build up around certain hobbies, as in the proverbial cafeteria room: jocks, nerds, pretty girls, geeks, theater kids, and other subgroups of students.

Church kids who grew up in Sunday school together will likely overcome this hurdle, but those who are newer to the group may not. This is especially true among visitors, unless the friend who brought the visitor is deliberate about introducing him or her to others in the group. No youth pastor wants these divisions to exist, and there are beautiful moments (usually during mission trips and service projects) when these divisions simply wash away. But unless you are intentional about unity, a youth group can splinter into these types of cliques.

The Difference Between a Clique and a Group of Friends

The most obvious reason cliques happen is because of friendship. As C. S. Lewis wrote, "The typical expression of opening Friendship would be something like, 'What? You too? I thought I was the only one.'"[14] This is a beautiful thing to happen, and it should be encouraged in our ministries. Why would we want to keep students from finding a Christian best friend with whom they can share deep fellowship through their teenage years? The problem is not with friendship, but with exclusivity.

These types of close friendships can pose two problems in youth ministry. First, the friends can seem so close with each other that it's intimidating to other students and makes them feel unwelcomed. Second, these friends can be so focused on their friendship that they actually are building walls between themselves and everyone else. While talking about cliques with students, be sure to emphasize that friendships are not the problem, exclusivity is.

Practical Guidance for Tearing Down Walls

- **Cast a vision for ministry.** Without understanding *why* you want them to be more others-minded, groups of friends will feel singled out and attacked. Casting a vision for a "culture of welcome" empowers students for ministry and deploys friend groups to serve others. It's also easier to separate them during group time when they know you are doing this to empower them to welcome others.
- **Use games and service projects.** These are times when students typically have their guard down and need to rely on one another. Separating friends at every opportunity will likely backfire. But creating moments for students in cliques to depend on those outside of their clique—to win a game or complete a project—will help erode walls.

- **Give specific feedback.** When talking with students about cliques, it helps to share real examples of times you have seen others feel unwelcomed. Do this without casting accusations or making them feel like you are judging their friendship. Calling a special meeting for this conversation will immediately make students defensive. Instead, keep this conversation in your back pocket until an opportunity presents itself, and then graciously and lovingly invite students to welcome others into their group. This usually works best as a personal conversation with one or two students, not with the whole group.

- **Identify a "man of peace" (or two) within the clique.** Very rarely will the leader of the clique catch a vision for tearing down walls and reaching out to those who have felt excluded. But there may be a student who can be a voice for change from within the group, if you can talk to that student about it. However, be careful that you do not pit friends against each other, lest you actually cause more division.

- **Give them the gospel.** The gospel unites students, regardless of how little else they have in common, so they are brothers and sisters in the family of God. Although cliques can be infuriating to the youth workers who are trying to build a welcoming and loving atmosphere for all students, it is important to remember that correction doesn't always require a hammer. These students need grace, not a harsh rebuke. You have a chance to display the Lord's patience and kindness by the way you talk with them and help them see the ways they have excluded others and caused hurt among the group. The gospel calls those on the outside (sinners) to become dearly loved children of God. This invitation is beautifully portrayed in youth ministry when students embrace a welcoming and gracious posture toward one another, recognizing that their bond doesn't come from external traits they share in common, but because of Christ: "We have fellowship with one another, and the blood of Jesus his Son cleanses us from all sin" (1 John 1:7).

36

Forming a Partnership with Parents

Parents matter. Sometimes youth workers forget this simple truth. It is strangely common for youth ministries to operate with parents only providing food and vehicles for the occasional event. Surely, a genuine partnership with parents is more than this.

The biblical witness is abundantly clear: parents are the primary disciple makers of the next generation. This is evident from God's instruction at creation to "be fruitful and multiply" (Genesis 1:28), through Moses's command to the people of Israel that "these commandments that I give you today are to be on your hearts. Impress them on your children" (Deuteronomy 6:6–7 NIV), and down to the New Testament's call for parents to bring children up "in the discipline and instruction of the Lord" (Ephesians 6:4). If a youth ministry is not actively seeking to equip parents to minister to their teenagers, it is overlooking the clearest biblical teaching about raising up the next generation in the faith.

Youth workers should be the greatest advocates for parents in the church. In many cases, the youth pastor is someone who is younger and has not personally raised teenagers. But many volunteer youth workers are parents with hard-won wisdom and encouragement to offer the other parents—and their voices need to be heard. If parents are not regularly involved in discussions about youth ministry, the youth workers are missing out on multiple fronts: cultivating trust, learning from each other, and encouraging parents to be their teens' spiritual leader.

EQUIPPING PARENTS TO EVANGELIZE AND DISCIPLE THEIR TEENAGERS

Above all else, parents need to be fluent in the gospel. The Deuteronomy 6 passage that Christians point to as direction for family discipleship begins with the verse Jesus calls the greatest commandment: "You shall love the LORD your God with all your heart and with all your soul and with all your might" (v. 5). The next verse says, "These words that I command you today shall be on your heart." This reflects the truth that parents cannot pass on to their kids what they themselves do not have.

If parents' faith is not clearly evident, or if they talk about grace but never show it, their kids will learn from that example. Family discipleship begins in the parents' hearts. The greatest thing parents can do for their kids' spiritual development is to prioritize their own spiritual maturity. And yet, parents do not need to "arrive" before they can start to shape their kids' faith. Even imperfect faith has a meaningful effect on kids when parents are open about their own faith journey.

This is also true of nonreligious parents. They too shape their children's spiritual development, but in a way that teaches the irrelevance of religion. Every youth pastor, regardless of his own age or family background, can help parents by encouraging them to grow in the gospel of grace. (More information on this topic is given in chapter 38, "Supporting Students from Unbelieving Families.")

The best kind of family discipleship trains kids to integrate their faith into all of life—friendship, recreation, education, work, media use, self-identity, etc. However, most Christian adults do not have this kind of faith themselves because they haven't been discipled either. Many parents of teenagers were raised in homes where faith was a highly private matter, so they have no frame of reference for what family discipleship might look like. The youth pastor and volunteers do not need to have all the answers, but they may need to create opportunities for seasoned parents who know how to practice discipleship to share their experience and wisdom with parents who don't.

Parents often will turn to youth workers for help understanding youth culture. They want to understand their teenager's world: what they are listening to and watching, the social media platforms they use, and the video games they play. Parents assume youth workers know more about youth culture than your typical adult does. Creating space to discuss youth culture, and highlighting resources or articles that help parents think biblically about youth culture, will only benefit your ministry. You can share these through regular newsletters, social media, and in-person meetings.

Finally, remember you are not the only one who cares about parents. Work with other ministry leaders to integrate family-discipleship training into the ministries parents already attend. For example, suggest that small-group leaders include questions that connect lessons with parenting. Finding ways to incorporate family discipleship into existing ministries is usually the most effective and sustainable way to equip parents.

BUILDING BLOCKS OF A HEALTHY PARTNERSHIP WITH PARENTS

1. **Understand their expectations.** Also help them understand the church's vision for their teenagers. If the parents and the youth ministry have different definitions of a successful youth ministry, there will be conflict ahead. Paint a picture of what gospel-centered youth ministry means to you, and give them space to ask questions and discuss it with the youth leaders.

2. **Seek their input.** Believe it or not, parents have some excellent ideas, some of which might be better than yours. Cast a vision for what you're trying to accomplish, and brainstorm together, especially when building the youth-group calendar. If the ministry is too large for all parents to

meet together and exchange ideas, you might recruit a small group of parents to serve as a parent board.

3. **Over-communicate.** Don't send one email and think you have communicated important information. With the amount of free communication tools at your disposal, an hour of effort each week should be ample time to create a weekly newsletter, update your page on the church website, and post announcements on social media. If this takes longer than an hour, it probably means you are still gathering the necessary information—in which case the need to create these communications will force you to get organized.

4. **Schedule multiple parent meetings each year.** Resist the temptation to make these meetings purely informational. If the meetings are purely about the youth group calendar, parents could get that information from your weekly newsletter and you're wasting their time, so they won't come to future meetings. Instead, provide space for teaching and discussion about what's happening in youth culture, or family discipleship, or other timely issues that would benefit parents. Some youth ministries even schedule meetings that run like a school's parent-teacher conferences, where parents meet with their teen's small-group leader to discuss the student's spiritual development.

5. **Do what you say you'll do.** Youth workers can be tempted to make commitments they don't mean in order to appease a parent who is upset or frustrated. But being a person of your word is one of the best ways to build trust, and empty promises are an easy way to lose credibility.

6. **Be honest.** If a student is struggling or misbehaving, talk with one of their parents. This doesn't need to be a disciplinary conversation. You might ask for advice on how to help their student have the youth group experience everyone wants for them. Perhaps their kid is going through something at school that's contributing to their behavior, or there could be something helpful a teacher does at school that you could implement at youth group.

7.   **Encourage them.** Parents should hear about it when their son or daughter does something especially thoughtful or kind. Don't exaggerate (because they know their kid enough to know when you're doing so), but you might see a side of the student they rarely see at home. Besides, if the only time you contact parents is to ask them for a favor or when their kids are in trouble, they might begin to view you with some degree of dread.

8.   **Pray for them and with them.** Whenever able, ask parents how you can be praying for them and for their family—and actually do it then and there. A special bond forms when people pray together. This also helps you remember to pray for them later, and if shows them you are serious about caring for their family. In the end, both the youth ministry and the family are completely reliant on the work of God in students' lives—so pray without ceasing.

37
Supporting Single-Parent Families

My parents divorced when I was entering middle school. As difficult as that season was, they did an incredible job shielding me from many of the common wounds students suffer when parents divorce. My youth pastor also played a pivotal role in my life by being someone I could talk to and cry with, and I knew he was praying for me. From his example, I have learned that the one of greatest things a youth worker can do is be a generous listener who will pray with you and lead you to Jesus when your world is falling apart.

Not all single-parent families are the same. While there are characteristics they share, a family where a parent recently passed away from cancer will have different felt needs than one where Dad was never in the picture. For this reason, it is important to consider different types of single-parent families and their needs.

REASONS FOR SINGLE-PARENT HOUSEHOLDS

- **Death.** Consider how long ago the parent passed away, and how it happened. A student whose father committed suicide or died from a drug overdose will cope differently than one who is grieving after a prolonged sickness or an accident. Only give hope of the deceased parent's eternal destiny if you know that parent was a professing Christian.

Still, the gospel is a message of life and hope for those who grieve. One practical expression of sustained care is to set a recurring annual reminder to check in with the family and make sure they know you have not forgotten their loss.

- **Divorce.** It is common for children of divorce to blame themselves for their parents' separation. Students who rarely see one parent anymore will be prone to struggle with abandonment issues and the need for approval. Be a generous listener who validates their feelings while pointing them to the faithfulness of God, who will never leave or abandon his children "My father and my mother have forsaken me, but the LORD will take me in" (Psalm 27:10).

- **Shared custody.** Shared custody can be a confusing situation with two parents who have very different values, house rules, and responses to God. In some unfortunate cases, children are used as pawns between parents, or even as informants. It is of utmost importance that youth workers avoid speaking poorly of either parent. Instead, offer a steadiness students are lacking while you help them see how their faith guides their lives regardless of whose house they are in.

- **Dad was never part of the family.** Students who grow up in single-parent households often take on adult responsibilities much sooner than their peers, especially if they have younger siblings. Some will find the description of God as their heavenly Father a great comfort, while others will assume this makes him unreliable. Invest in these students, not as a surrogate parent but as a spiritual aunt or uncle.

HELPING STUDENTS NAVIGATE DIVORCE

- **Be available.** The ministry of presence is a real thing. Showing up speaks volumes, especially to a student with a parent who isn't able to attend sporting events or special school programs due to the pressures of parenting alone.

- **Listen.** These students are hurting and need to know you will listen to them if they open up. I remember word-vomiting things to my youth pastor that I hadn't expressed to anyone else simply because I knew he would listen without invalidating my feelings.

- **Be a mentor.** The Lord will provide opportunities to step in and speak truth—take them. Remember that sometimes gentle words can be so gentle they become unclear. Godly mentors speak clearly and directly but with compassion and humility. If the student needs to be corrected, do it with dignity and grace. If the student needs to be comforted, do it without fluffiness. Embrace the opportunity to be an authority figure, but with the heart of a spiritual uncle or aunt.
- **Don't give up on them.** Students from single-parent families may push you away. Perhaps they are testing you to see if you'll abandon them easily, or maybe they've simply constructed emotional barricades to protect themselves from being hurt by another adult leaving them. Whatever their reason, be persistent. Keep showing up. Keep calling.
- **Proclaim God as the perfect parent.** When you talk about God our heavenly Father, highlight that he is the only perfect parent. Our earthly parents are imperfect shadows who point to the perfect Father of the people of God.

SUPPORTING SINGLE PARENTS

- **Check in regularly.** Many single parents work irregular hours, sometimes even needing to work multiple jobs. They will have a difficult time participating in parent meetings and other youth group events. Without taking initiative, you may never even meet them! Send them an email, make the phone call, schedule a conversation over coffee at their convenience (and offer to pay).
- **Be reliable, but don't overpromise.** The last thing a single parent needs from a youth worker is to wonder whether or not you will do what you say. Being a person of your word is a powerful expression of love and helpfulness to a parent who is already working hard to hold things together.

- **Acknowledge their shame (but not publicly!).** When single parents show up to parent meetings or family ministry events, they often experience a deep sense of shame. This is a gnawing feeling that whispers, "You don't belong here. You aren't like the other parents here." When you know this devilish whisper exists, you will be better equipped to highlight the mercy of God which has removed our shame through Jesus Christ. The best way to acknowledge this is silently. Simply care for these precious parents in a way that says, "I see you. You completely belong here."
- **Offer scholarships without pity.** No one likes feeling like a charity case, but it is likely that single-parent households struggle financially. As much as possible, have a scholarship fund available for camps and special events, and work to offer it in a way that doesn't make the parent feel shame.
- **Provide real help.** Some families struggle to complete tasks that used to be done by the parent who is no longer present. This could be anything from landscaping to cooking meals. Reach out to the remaining parent to help meet their practical needs, being careful to hold a genuine posture of brotherly love rather than pity.

God: The Perfect Parent

Family is a living metaphor for the eternal family of God.[15] Accordingly, it is common for children from fractured families to carry their parental hurts into their relationship with God. For example, children whose father was emotionally distant will often struggle to experience intimacy in their relationship with God. Or students whose fathers were emotionally available but struggled with financial provisions may feel the loving kindness of Christ but struggle to trust him to provide for them in "real life." Discipleship of students from single-family households will include talking them through the ways their relationship with their parents affects their relationship with God.

The faithfulness of God is more than some cliché students hear about in Sunday school. The steadfast love of God is a recurring theme throughout the Bible. He does not abandon his children or leave them without hope. In love, God sent his Son to rescue sinners so they would be adopted as sons and daughters of God (John 1:12). As children of God, we are heirs to a glorious inheritance (Romans 8:17). Jesus assured his disciples of his unfailing presence through the indwelling Holy Spirit, telling them, "I will not leave you as orphans" (John 14:18). The Bible's portrayal of God as our Father in heaven proclaims that his intimate love for his children is the bedrock of Christian faith. Regardless of their family of origin, the cross is an enduring reminder of their lasting family, and of their Father's faithfulness to draw them near.

38

Supporting Students from Unbelieving Families

Youth ministry is often one of the more evangelistic ministries in a church. A youth group is often composed of both students who grew up in the church and those whose families are hesitant about their teenager attending anything hosted in a church. Thankfully, both unchurched teenagers and lifelong church kids need to hear the gospel proclaimed and applied regularly. But the range of spiritual background still requires careful nuance.

Youth ministry is about raising up a new generation in the gospel. One of the greatest honors a youth worker receives is getting a front-seat to watch a previously unreached family encounter the saving grace of Jesus Christ. There are unique ways to minister to students from these families, as well as some pitfalls to avoid.

WAYS TO HELP STUDENTS FROM NON-CHRISTIAN FAMILIES

- **Don't assume Bible knowledge.** Statements like, "I'm sure you all know this verse" only serve to make these students feel like they don't belong. Don't get bogged down explaining everything and everyone, but be sure to define important words and people in your messages.

- **Articulate the gospel.** This should be true at all times, but youth workers shouldn't assume students know what we mean when we mention "the gospel." Instead, proclaim it clearly and consistently so every student hears and can respond with faith-fueled repentance. Be very clear about who Jesus is, what Jesus did, and what he has promised to those who have faith in him. Preaching the gospel with clarity means being aware of the assumptions students make about God—especially the presumptions that if God is love he would never judge anyone.

- **Help them count the cost.** Rather than pressing for immediate decisions, encourage students to count the cost of following Jesus. Trusting in Jesus reaps eternal rewards, but the Christian life is often marked by trials and persecution. This is especially important if students may face opposition to their new faith at home. If you present the gospel as a message that is going to fix everything in their lives, it shouldn't be surprising when those students walk away from the faith after life gets (or remains) difficult. Students should be prepared to face some trials when their non-Christian family hears that they have converted to Christianity.

- **Teach them to study the Bible.** Developing a regular Bible-reading habit is the best way for students to nourish their faith. This is especially true of teenagers from non-Christian families whose parents and siblings will not provide spiritual encouragement. Their freedom to participate in youth group programs like Bible studies or discipleship groups may also be limited, so teaching them how to study on their own is especially important.

- **Encourage them to honor their parents and love their siblings.** Growing as a peacemaker can be one of the best ways for new Christians to display the gospel to their family. Families see the real us. When the gospel brings true change in a teenager, it will become evident to parents and siblings. Even when parents and siblings don't understand or agree with their newfound faith, they may grow to respect it because of the change they observe.

- **Give them a long-term perspective.** When students' lives are changed, there is great potential for transformation in the entire family. But this may take years. Encourage them not to grow discouraged when family is resistant, but to be faithful over the long haul.

LANDMINES TO AVOID WITH STUDENTS FROM NON-CHRISTIAN FAMILIES

- **Avoid evangelism that condemns.** One of the trickiest tightropes to walk in ministry has to do with teenagers from non-Christian families who become Christians. The gospel can sound more like a curse unto damnation than an invitation to eternal life when students become overly zealous in their evangelism of family members. It is likely these students are gravely concerned about eternal judgment resting on their family members—and that urgency is good. But youth workers will want to encourage students also to embrace patience that flows from confidence in God's sovereignty and grace that shapes the tone of evangelism.

- **Avoid pitting students against their parents.** Especially if the parents have religious convictions, they may respond the same way Christian parents would if their kids were being converted to any other religion. It helps to remember that parents usually want what is best for their students, and if youth workers are able to come alongside and support the entire family, they have a much higher chance of effective ministry. Earning a family's trust takes deliberate effort over a period of time. A simple introductory conversation when you give them your cell phone number can go a long way toward building a healthy relationship with parents.

- **Avoid overstepping personal boundaries.** Coaches and teachers don't usually contact students outside of activities, so parents' warning bells can be triggered by well-intentioned youth workers who do. Recognize that parents may not be comfortable with the kind of relational ministry familiar to churchgoers. It is best to err on the side of caution, especially while you're still building trust. Do your best to avoid private conversations that could give the appearance of inappropriate motives.

- **Don't be ignorant of cultural and religious differences.** When a student's family practices another religion or is from a traditionally non-Christian culture, there will likely be an elevated measure of opposition to the student's newfound faith in Jesus. Help students honor their parents and traditions as much as possible without engaging in practices that are contrary to Christ.

- **Don't keep them confined to youth group.** A church where adults genuinely care about teenagers can be a powerful witness to unchurched students, who likely assume the older generation is cold and uninterested in them. Encourage the whole church to serve as a surrogate spiritual family. Don't underestimate the impact this can make on a student.

39

Responding to Criticism

Whenever there is a leader, there will be critics. Even if you are a volunteer youth worker and not the youth pastor, you have likely experienced the sting of criticism against you or your team. Some of the best ministry lessons are learned from criticism, so not all criticism is bad and not all critics are haters. But at the same time, some of the most painful moments that will make you want to give up on church will come from the mouths of critics.

Jesus taught his disciples, "Bless those who curse you, pray for those who abuse you" (Luke 6:28). Although critics are not always cursers or abusers, it still can be painful to receive correction and therefore tempting to respond with anger or resentment. As men and women who are discipling the next generation, our response to criticism is sanctifying—it teaches us to practice the grace and patience we have received through Christ—while also being a godly example to students and parents. Youth workers often try to teach students about submitting to authority and having a teachable spirit. Consider criticism you receive an opportunity to lead by example in front of your students.

TYPES OF CRITICS
Some critics you will face in ministry are well-intentioned while others are literally trying to get you kicked out of the youth

ministry. Critique can be hard to hear but often proves helpful, so try to discern what type of critic you're talking with so you know how to respond.

- People who are hurt or angry
- People who think they could do your job better than you
- Parents who are advocating for their teenager
- Parents who want you to fix the ministry so their kids will want to attend
- People who are genuinely trying to help you grow and improve
- People in leadership (perhaps the youth pastor, an elder, or another supervisor) who initiate a hard conversation about a weakness in your ministry

RESPONDING TO CRITICISM WITH GRACE

- **Recognize that disagreements are part of leadership.** Great leaders also have critics. The only leaders who do not have critics are those who are so toxic people would rather leave than voice disagreement. Resisting critique may protect your ego, but it also robs you of the opportunity to learn from others and it tells them their opinions don't matter. Criticism, when offered with sincerity and received with humility, can be a gift to your own personal development and to the ministry's fruitfulness.
- **Listen for the truth.** If you always assume your critics are wrong, you will never learn anything new. Even if the criticism is mean-spirited and based on bad information, there is always something to learn. At the very least, you can discover how some people are perceiving you or the ministry.
- **Ask questions to uncover the heart of their critique.** It is common for the criticism that falls on youth workers to be a smokescreen for a bigger concern. For instance, if a few parents overreact to an event that bombed, this tells

you something about their frustration with the ministry in general and opens the door for a bigger (and more important!) conversation. You might say something like, "I can't promise to do everything you want, but if I did, what would that look like?" Their response (or lack of response) could lead to a constructive conversation about the real disagreements at hand.

- **Be slow to defend yourself.** If you immediately defend yourself, it will almost always make you look guilty. Your tone, posture, and nonverbals will often determine whether the criticism becomes a conflict or a fruitful conversation. If you are accused, it is usually best to answer questions you are asked while allowing others to defend you.

- **Speak directly, with humility.** Prioritize clarity and kindness, even when you need to say something hard that may not be well-received. Humility does not mean you never tell a critic they're wrong about you. It means you don't speak with a self-righteous spirit and are truly open to receiving correction as a chance to learn and grow. There are times when critics need to hear you clearly and directly say, "No, we are not going to do that" or "Thank you for your perspective, but I think you are wrong." However, if this is all you ever say to critics, you need to evaluate your heart and listen to what they have to say more carefully.

- **Avoid blame-shifting.** As a volunteer youth worker, it can be easy to escape the criticism by pointing the critic to someone else. Be a team player and stand by your team the same way you would hope they'd stand by you, even if you disagree with what they've done. If you can't do this, you have become the person-who-thinks-they-can-do-your-job-better-than-you critic referenced above.

- **Encourage critics to talk with the person the critique is about.** In Matthew 18:15–17, Jesus gives direct teaching about going to fellow believers when they have wronged you. Even when the criticism isn't about a personal wrong, this passage shows the importance of talking directly to the person involved. If Christians belong to the family of faith, they should give one another enough mutual respect to have a personal conversation about the matter at hand. If the critic is not willing to do this, they are proving themselves to be the worst kind of critic—one who wants to tell others what to do without any commitment to be part of the solution.

• **Have friends who pray for you.** Receiving criticism about ministry can wound your heart in surprisingly deep ways that you never anticipated when you signed up to serve teenagers. Gossip is sinful and wrong, but if something has been said to you that cut your heart deeply, talk about it with a trusted friend or mentor. Receive the care and prayer you need to process the incident well. Without this intervention, many leaders experience serious stress in ministry that can hinder both their spiritual health and ministry for years to come.

When criticism comes your way, remember that you have been perfectly loved and fully accepted by the grace of Jesus Christ. Although the critic may not accept you, God does—and he has. This freedom and confidence in Christ is what enables you to receive correction in a godly manner. Insecure people can't handle rebuke, but you are firm in your standing before God.

40

Boundaries, Confidentiality, and Mandated Reporting

Keeping students safe includes maintaining healthy boundaries, showing discernment about what conversations to keep confidential, and being aware of protection policies. This is an important element to youth ministry because students learn from more than the words we speak; they learn from our example. If that example does not align with the messages we teach, they will believe our actions instead of our words.

The Bible speaks frequently about God's heart for the vulnerable. Faithful youth workers advocate for these students and sacrifice joyfully so they can see God's redeeming love displayed for them. Boundaries, confidentiality, and child-protection laws may not be the most exciting reasons people sign up to serve in youth ministry. These inconveniences reflect a gospel-driven commitment to seek and save the lost. But they are important, and they free volunteers up to serve with clear expectations.

BOUNDARIES EVERY YOUTH WORKER SHOULD EMBRACE

- **Act like a mentor, not a peer.** Embracing the role of a mentor will help guide your interactions and conversations with students. Youth workers who behave like students are not good youth workers.

- **Avoid one-on-one meetings in private spaces.** If you are meeting with a student, regardless of gender, make sure you are somewhere public or easily seen by others. This is inconvenient, but it helps ensure your ministry to students can continue for the long haul.
- **Inform others about one-on-one meetings.** Tell someone— your youth pastor, a spouse, the student's parents—to make sure these conversations are not happening in secret. This doesn't mean disclosing everything about the conversation when it's over, but secret meetings with students can easily take a wrong turn.
- **Guard your social media feeds.** Adults whose social media accounts include students should practice extra discernment about what they post and share. Posting questionable pictures and content is a legitimately easy way to be disqualified to serve in youth ministry. Churches and youth ministries may also want to discuss parameters for youth workers being friends with students on certain networks that rely on privacy, like Snapchat.
- **Limit personal touch.** Students need a personal touch, so eliminating all touch may protect youth workers from accusation but come at great cost to caring for the whole person. Your policy on regular personal touches should be discussed among your ministry team in order to decide what is best for your particular community. Your church's child protection policy may also have specific guidance about personal contact. When meeting one-on-one with a student, be especially careful about personal touch and proximity to the student.
- **Coordinate carpools among parents.** Driving students home is a normal part of some youth ministries, and yet it is often the time and place when youth workers are most at risk for ending up alone with a student. Making an effort to coordinate carpools among parents will not only safeguard youth leaders, it can also provide additional time for students to bond with other students who live nearby.

- **Avoid rough play.** It can be tempting to bond with the youth group guys by wrestling and other rough play. Although it may seem harmless, there is a strong chance that some students have a history of domestic violence and may be triggered. This can make them feel unsafe at church, the place where they should feel most secure in relationships with godly men and women.

CONFIDENTIALITY

One of the best pieces of advice I got when I was entering youth ministry was this: Never promise confidentiality. Instead, tell students, "If you trust me enough to tell me, trust me enough to know whether or not I need to tell someone else."

Of course, students will feel betrayed if youth workers relay every conversation to parents. Youth workers who are prone to gossip will quickly ruin their trustworthiness. At the same time, it is important to convey to students that circumstances may require us to tell someone else what they've said.

One of the best ways to discern what conversations to keep private and what conversations to share with parents, the pastor, or the police is captured by the word *crisis*. If there is a situation on the verge of spiraling into a serious problem, it is best to encourage the student to discuss the matter with their parents. Offering to be present to mediate such conversations can reassure the student they are not being left to figure things out alone. If after such prodding students continue to resist seeking help, it may be time to break confidences because of your concern for the student. And if the crisis is urgent, it must be addressed swiftly and with courage. Make the hard phone call to the youth pastor in order to pass the information up the chain of command to the church's official mandated reporter to the police. There will be state guidelines for that person to follow.

Volunteer youth workers will see and hear things the youth pastor won't. If there is something of concern or urgency, be sure to discuss it rather than assume the youth pastor already knows.

It's better to hear it from multiple sources than risk remaining unaware. Once again, this might not need to involve all the details, but when there is conflict between students or concerns within a family it is important to inform the youth pastor. Youth workers who are concerned that these conversations turn them into gossips need to remember that gossip is talking about others behind their back for the sake of entertainment. These conversations, however, are taking place in order to help bring healing and peace.

MANDATED REPORTING

Volunteer youth workers are considered mandated reporters in most states because they are leaders in the church who are working with minors. This means youth workers are legally liable if they fail to report information about abuse to the authorities. Details and protocol vary by state, but it is essential for youth workers to know the law and follow it in order to protect the teenagers in their care. In most cases, volunteer youth workers should report firsthand accounts of abuse, threats of abuse, or suicidal ideas to their supervisor, who is then responsible to file an official report as mandated by state law. Secondhand accounts should not be overlooked, but they are not usually mandated-report situations.

As the last few years have shown, churches have a regrettable track record of dealing with cases of abuse in-house rather than reporting those incidents to the local authorities. May this be a time for youth workers to recognize this has been wrong and has not protected students. Following the law should be the church's bare minimum, not the ceiling for how to respond to crises.

Finally, if your church does not have an official child protection policy, gather a team of leaders to write one in the coming six months. Call a few churches in your community to request their policies as samples, contact your church's insurance company for their requirements and suggestions, and then start a review process with a team of nursery workers, children's ministry workers, youth ministry workers, and parents. It is better to have a broad policy that you keep than an overly-specific policy you often break. Your church is liable to do what is written in the child protection policy. An effective policy will likely require revisions every few years and will lead to some difficult changes in the various ministries in the church. But it ensures that children are protected, parents are set at ease, and volunteers have clear expectations.

BASIC ELEMENTS OF A CHILD PROTECTION POLICY

- Short summary of your church's intent behind the policy
- Definitions of abuse and signs of abuse
- Listing of ministries within the church that should abide by this policy
- Safety protocols: number of adults required, bathroom policies, guidelines on one-on-one car transportation, background check requirements, etc. (Note: sometimes these are listed generally for all ministries, and other times they are given as distinct protocols for children's ministry and for youth ministry.)
- Reporting protocols: how to determine if a report is necessary, who will give the report

Youth workers are sometimes called to minister to students who are living in extraordinarily difficult circumstances. There are far more students who have suffered abuse or neglect than youth workers realize. At the same time, churches have been known to cover up incidents of abuse, thus bringing suspicion and mistrust upon the bride of Christ. These protocols go unnoticed by the majority of students. But those who come from challenging backgrounds can find comfort in knowing their safety is valued in your ministry. This speaks volumes to vulnerable students and displays God's compassion, which invites them to be reconciled and adopted as dearly loved children of God through faith in Jesus Christ. As you lead students to Jesus, remember those who have been deeply wounded, and care for them with the Lord's tender love. By establishing and maintaining proper boundaries and protocols, you are showing them dignity and compassion that flows out of God's gospel love.

Conclusion:
Playing the Long Game
in Youth Ministry

If you have served in youth ministry for even a few weeks, you know what it's like to drive home and wonder if you just wasted your time. Discouragement can come from your own insecurities ("I'm too old, boring, serious"), or frustration with the students ("they're too disrespectful, cliquey, apathetic"), or it can pertain to the youth ministry's leadership ("the youth pastor is too disorganized, aloof, demanding"). Resist the temptation to be drawn into discouragement. Your ministry is important and the Holy Spirit is at work in ways that your eyes cannot perceive.

When discouragement abounds, let this be a reminder of Jesus's words in Matthew 9:37–38, "The harvest is plentiful, but the laborers are few; therefore pray earnestly to the Lord of the harvest to send out laborers into his harvest." It is the Lord's harvest. It is his ministry. As you labor in the field of youth ministry, remember that you serve in the Lord's field, leading his children home. The harvest does not rest squarely on your shoulders. Trust the faithfulness of God to bear lasting fruit through your ministry. After all, if you believe salvation and sanctification are gifts of the Holy Spirit, then youth ministry is a chance to put that faith to action!

One of the most helpful reminders that has sustained my zeal for youth ministry when I feel like giving up is simply this: I'm playing the long game. If your small group time was a train wreck, then dust yourself off, pray for your students, and keep showing up to play the long game. If you say the wrong thing to a kid and they stop talking to you, then don't give up on them; apologize and keep playing the long game. If you're new and feel like giving up because it's taking a while to connect with students, know that making a sustained effort to establish trust is a necessary part of thriving in youth ministry. Discouragement can harden your heart to the work of God that you simply cannot see, or it can be a cattle prod that drives you to prayerful endurance as you lead students to Jesus.

Youth ministry has high highs and low lows. Remember that the mission of youth ministry is to build adult disciples whose faith took root during their teen years. That's the goal. Endure. Pray. Lean on your team. Keep your eyes on Jesus.

Acknowledgments

Thank you to my wife, Tracy, and my kids, Matthew and Hannah. Much of this book was written during quarantine due to the COVID-19 pandemic, and you sacrificed significant time for me to spend at my computer. Your encouragement and support are the fuel behind every page in this book. And thanks to my mother and father for always supporting me in my ministry endeavors.

It has been a true pleasure to work with the team at New Growth Press. Barbara Juliani, Cheryl White, and Ruth Castle have given considerable support for this project. Jack Klumpenhower's edits made this book tighter and more useful.

Many friends offered extremely helpful feedback on various chapters, but especially Kevin, Clark, Anna, and Liz. A special thanks goes to my Rooted Ministry family—I have learned so much from you about gospel-centered youth ministry.

Finally, this book wouldn't exist without my amazing team of youth workers at South Shore Baptist Church. You were the original audience for this book and helped me select what topics to include as chapters. Many youth workers will benefit from your contributions to this project. Thank you!

Additional Resources

In all things, we want to give students the gospel. Inclusion in this list does not imply complete agreement, but I affirm each of these to be a trustworthy resource as you continue to lead students to Jesus.

Youth Ministry

Clark, Chap, *Adoptive Church: Creating an Environment Where Emerging Generations Belong* (Grand Rapids, MI: Baker, 2018).

Cole, Cameron and Jon Nielson, *Gospel-Centered Youth Ministry: A Practical Guide* (Wheaton, IL: Crossway, 2016).

McGarry, Michael, *A Biblical Theology of Youth Ministry: Teenagers in the Life of the Church* (Nashville, TN: Randall House, 2019).

Talbot, Christopher, *Remodeling Youth Ministry: A Biblical Blueprint for Ministering to Students* (Gallatin, TN: Welch College Press, 2017).

Teaching and Preaching

Fields, Doug and Duffy Robbins, *Speaking to Teenagers: How to Think About, Create, and Deliver Effective Messages* (Grand Rapids, MI: Zondervan, 2007).

Helm, David, *Expositional Preaching: How We Speak God's Word Today* (Wheaton, IL: Crossway, 2014).

Keller, Timothy, *Preaching: Communicating Faith in an Age of Skepticism* (New York: Penguin, 2015).

Discipleship

Helm, David, *One-to-One Bible Reading: A Simple Guide for Every Christian* (Kingsford, Australia: Matthias Media, 2010).

Hill, Drew, *Alongside: Loving Teenagers with the Gospel* (Greensboro, NC: New Growth Press, 2018).

Packer, J. I. and Gary Parrett, *Grounded in the Gospel: Building Believers the Old-Fashioned Way* (Grand Rapids, MI: Baker, 2010).

Youth Culture & Issues

Evangelical Alliance, *Trans Formed: A Brief Biblical and Pastoral Introduction to Understanding Transgender in a Changing Culture* (London, UK: Evangelical Alliance, 2018). Accessed 11/20/20, https://www.eauk.org/assets/files/downloads/Transformed.pdf

Kinnaman, David and Mark Matlock, *Faith for Exiles: 5 Ways for a New Generation to Follow Jesus in Digital Babylon* (Grand Rapids, MI: Baker, 2019).

Moore, Russell, *Onward: Engaging the Culture Without Losing the Gospel* (Nashville, TN: B&H Publishing, 2015).

Mueller, Walt, *Engaging the Soul of Youth Culture: Bridging Teen Worldviews and Christian Truth* (Downers Grove, IL: InterVarsity, 2006). Although this book's youth culture references have become somewhat dated, the principles about how to interpret and respond to youth culture have kept their value.

Perry, Jackie Hill, *Gay Girl, Good God: The Story of Who I Was, and Who God Has Always Been* (Nashville, TN: B&H Publishing, 2018).

Yuan, Christopher, *Holy Sexuality and the Gospel: Sex, Desire, and Relationships Shaped by God's Grand Story* (Colorado Springs, CO: Multnomah, 2018).

Gospel Centrality

Clowney, Edmund, *The Unfolding Mystery: Discovering Christ in the Old Testament* (Phillipsburg, NJ: P&R, 1988, 2013).

Goldsworthy, Graeme, *According to Plan: The Unfolding Revelation of God in the Bible* (Downers Grove, IL: InterVarsity, 2002).

Wilson, Jared C., *The Gospel-Driven Church: Uniting Church Growth Dreams with Metrics of Grace* (Grand Rapids, MI: Zondervan, 2019).

Apologetics

Cooper, Barry, *Can I Really Trust the Bible? And Other Questions about Scripture, Truth, and How God Speaks* (Charlotte, NC: The Good Book Company, 2014).

Köstenberger, Andreas, Darrell Bock, and Josh Chatraw, *Truth Matters: Confident Faith in a Confusing World* (Nashville, TN: B&H Publishing, 2014).

McLaughlin, Rebecca, *Confronting Christianity: 12 Hard Questions for the World's Largest Religion* (Wheaton, IL: Crossway, 2019).

Books for Students

Crowe, Jaquelle, *This Changes Everything: How the Gospel Transforms the Teen Years* (Wheaton, IL: Crossway, 2017).

Gilbert, Greg, *What Is the Gospel?* (Wheaton, IL: Crossway, 2010).

Hatton, Kristen, *Facetime: Your Identity in a Selfie World* (Greensboro, NC: New Growth Press, 2017).

Millar, Gary, *Need to Know: Your Guide to the Christian Life* (Charlotte, NC: The Good Book Company, 2020).

Thornton, Champ, *Radically Different: A Student's Guide to Community* (Greensboro, NC: New Growth Press, 2019).

Thune, Robert H. and Will Walker, *The Gospel-Centered Life for Teens* (Greensboro, NC: New Growth Press, 2014).

Generally Trustworthy Curriculum

Rooted Reservoir Curriculum
YouthMinistry360's *The Thread*
Lifeway's *The Gospel Project*
Reformed Youth Ministry Bible Studies
LeaderTreks's *Devotional Theology*

Online Resources

Got Questions. www.gotquestions.com. A helpful website with answers to nearly every Bible-related question students might ask.

Rooted Ministry. www.rootedministry.com. A ministry committed to empowering parents and youth workers to minister to students in light of the gospel of grace. Rooted hosts a parents blog, a youth workers blog, a podcast network, an annual conference, and local networks around the country.

The Center for Parent/Youth Understanding. www.cpyu. org. Resources on thinking Christianly about youth culture.

Reformed Youth Ministry (RYM). www.rym.org/. Provides many free resources on their site for youth workers and hosts annual conferences for students and youth workers.

Endnotes

1. Josh McDowell, *God-Breathed: The Undeniable Power and Reliability of Scripture* (Uhrichsville, OH: Barbour Publishing, 2015). This is an excellent resource for further study of the historical reliability of the Bible.

2. Most famously, see Tacitus's *Annals* 14.44 and Josephus's *Antiquities* 18.3.3.

3. Aaron Earls, "Most Teenagers Drop Out of Church as Young Adults," Lifeway Research, January 15, 2019, https://lifewayresearch.com/2019/01/15/most-teenagers-drop-out-of-church-as-young-adults/.

4. For more on adaptation and evolution within species, see Jonathan Sarfati, *Refuting Evolution: A Handbook for Students, Parents, and Teachers Countering the Latest Arguments for Evolution* (Atlanta, GA: Creation Book Publishers, 2008).

5. This view is most famously presented by Meredith G. Kline in *Kingdom Prologue: Genesis Foundations for a Covenantal Worldview* (Eugene, OR: Wipf and Stock, 2006).

6. Juliana Menasce Horowitz and Nikki Graf, "Most U.S. Teens See Anxiety and Depression as a Major Problem Among Their Peers," Pew Research Center, February 20, 2019, https://www.pewsocialtrends.org/2019/02/20/most-u-s-teens-see-anxiety-and-depression-as-a-major-problem-among-their-peers/.

7. This chapter is adapted, with permission, from a post I wrote for the Rooted Ministry blog, "Suffering and Sovereignty: How to Help Your Students Embrace the Tension," Rooted Ministry, January 28, 2020, https://www.rootedministry.com/blog/suffering-and-sovereignty-how-to-help-your-students-embrace-the-tension/.

8. For more on discipling relationships in the church, see my book, *A Biblical Theology of Youth Ministry: Teenagers in the Life of the Church* (Nashville, TN: Randall House, 2019).

9. Lawrence Richards, "A Four Step Strategy for Teaching Students," http://smeonline.net/wp-content/uploads/Hook-Book-Look-Took-4-part-Strategy-for-Teaching.pdf.

10. See Jean M. Twenge, *iGen: Why Today's Super-Connected Kids Are Growing Up Less Rebellious, More Tolerant, Less Happy—and Completely Unprepared for Adulthood—and What That Means for the Rest of Us* (New York: Atria Books, 2017).

11. The Barna Group, *Gen Z: The Culture, Beliefs and Motivations Shaping the Next Generation* (Ventura, CA: Barna Group, 2018), 46–47.

12. "What's the Average Age of a Child's First Exposure to Porn?" Fight the New Drug, January 28, 2020, https://fightthenewdrug.org/real-average-age-of-first-exposure/.

13. Ken Sande, *The Peacemaker: A Biblical Guide to Resolving Personal Conflict* (Grand Rapids, MI: Baker, 1991).

14. C. S. Lewis, *The Four Loves* (Orlando, FL: Harcourt Brace & Company, 1960), 65.

15. This is explored in exegetical and theological depth in my book, *A Biblical Theology of Youth Ministry*, 99–110.